CHAIN AND ANCHOR MAKING IN THE BLACK COUNTRY

RON MOSS

SUTTON PUBLISHING

Sutton Publishing Limited
Phoenix Mill · Thrupp · Stroud
Gloucestershire · GL5 2BU

First published 2006

Title page photograph: One of the fires or teams of chain-makers that made anchor chain for the *Titanic.* It is $3\frac{3}{8}$in in diameter and twenty-two lengths of 15 fathoms were made for this order.

British Library Cataloguing in Publication Data
A catalogue record for this book is available from the British Library.

ISBN 0-7509-4221-5

Typeset in 10.5/13.5 Plantin.

Printed and bound in England by
J.H. Haynes & Co. Ltd, Sparkford.

Unless otherwise noted, all photographs are from the author's collection.

THE BLACK COUNTRY SOCIETY

The Black Country Society is proud to be associated with **Sutton Publishing** of Stroud. In 1994 the society was invited by Sutton Publishing to collaborate in what has proved to be a highly successful publishing partnership, namely the extension of the ***Britain in Old Photographs*** series into the Black Country. In this joint venture the Black Country Society has played an important role in establishing and developing a major contribution to the region's photographic archives by encouraging society members to compile books of photographs of the area or town in which they live.

The first book in the Black Country series was *Wednesbury in Old Photographs* by Ian Bott, launched by Lord Archer of Sandwell in November 1994. Since then almost 70 Black Country titles have been published. The total number of photographs contained in these books is in excess of 13,000, suggesting that the whole collection is probably the largest regional photographic survey of its type in any part of the country to date.

This voluntary society was founded in 1967 as a reaction to the trends of the late 1950s and early '60s. This was a time when the reorganisation of local government was seen as a threat to the identity of individual communities and when, in the name of progress and modernisation, the industrial heritage of the Black Country was in danger of being swept away.

The general aims of the society are to stimulate interest in the past, present and future of the Black Country, and to secure at regional and national levels an accurate understanding and portrayal of what constitutes the Black Country and, wherever possible, to encourage and facilitate the preservation of the Black Country's heritage.

The society, which now has over 2,500 members worldwide, organises a yearly programme of activities. There are six venues in the Black Country where evening meetings are held on a monthly basis from September to April. In the summer months, there are fortnightly guided evening walks in the Black Country and its green borderland, and there is also a full programme of excursions further afield by car. Details of all these activities are to be found on the society's website, **www.blackcountrysociety.co.uk**, and in ***The Blackcountryman***, the quarterly magazine that is distributed to all members.

PO Box 71 · Kingswinford · West Midlands DY6 9YN

Note: Sums of money mentioned in the text are given in pre-decimal pounds, shillings and pence (*£ s d*). There were 12 pence to the shilling and 20 shillings to the pound; larger amounts were sometimes given in guineas (1 guinea = £1 1*s*). Conversions of some common amounts are as follows: 1*d* = 0.4p; 1p = 2.4*d*; 1*s* = 5p; 2*s* 6*d* = 12.5p. For weights, 1 pound (lb) = 0.45kg; 28lb = 1 quarter (qr); 4qr or 112lb = 1 hundredweight (cwt); and 20cwt = 1 ton.

Contents

Chapter 1 Chains and Anchors: Early History 1

Early Anchors 4; The Chained Library, Hereford Cathedral 4; Ancient Chains 6; Early Defence Chains 8; Development of the Modern Chain Industry 11; Slave Chains from the Past 12; The Location of Chain-Makers in Great Britain 14

Chapter 2 The Hand-Made Chain of the Black Country 19

Flat Winding Chain 19; Hancock's Chain 20; Round Bar Chain 25; Trade Unions 28; The Minimum Wage and the Chain Industry 32; Mary Macarthur and the 1910 'Lock-Out' 36; Women in the Chain Industry 40; Training for the Trade 44; Children in Chain-Shops 47; The Crowley Industrial Empire 48; Children in Workshops 51; Outworkers 55

Chapter 3 Chain Shops, Tools, Techniques and Testing 61

The Denholms: A Remarkable Iron-Forging Family 64; Fuel for the Hearth: Breeze 69; Tools of the Trade 72; The Oliver 72; The Tommy Hammer 78; Joining the Links 78; Dollied Chain 82; Proving or Testing Chain 85; Hemp and Iron Cables 86; Calculating Chain Strength 88; Test Certificates 89; British Chain-Makers in Germany 90; Standardisation 93; The Strength of a Chain-Link 97; Studs 99; Integral Stud Cable-Chain 105; Machine-Made Chain 107; Small-Chain 109; Large Cable-Chain 112; Tayco Chain 113; Blaco Chain 115; Lugless Chain-Joining Shackle or Kenter Shackle 118

Chapter 4 Anchors and Anchor Making 119

Forging Ships' Anchors 120; Developing Anchor Designs 127; The 'Modern' Stocked Anchor 129; Stockless Anchors 129; The Queens 130; Hall's Patent Anchor 134

Index 138

Chapter 1

Chains and Anchors: Early History

Chain has several meanings but is usually interpreted as a series of objects or things joined together. The chain that we concentrate on in this book consists of a series of rings, ovals or items of any other shape that are interlocked to form a strong flexible connection that can be used for retaining, binding, holding, hoisting or supporting objects. Another form can be used for transmitting or transferring power or drive. Chain in this sense is not to be confused with various units of measurement such as a Gunter's chain, which is a unit of length equal to 22yd, or an engineer's chain, a unit of length equal to 100ft, or a nautical chain, a unit of length equal to 15ft.

Chain-links can be made out of any material, particularly metal or plastic; many marvellous examples have been made of wood to show off the carpenter or wood carver's skills, because in order to finish with the links interlocked, they usually have to be made from one piece of wood. I have a photograph of a continuous wooden chain 132ft long, containing 1,123 links and with a hook on each end, that was carved out of a plank of wood 1ft long and 1¼in thick using only a pocket knife. This feat was carried out by a Mr Edward Buckley of Cannock at the start of the twentieth century; it is on show at the Heritage Centre in Lichfield. I have heard of several examples of chain carving like this.

Chain in various forms has been made and used by mankind for thousands of years. The first length of chain would probably have been made not long after it was discovered that metals could be worked into useful shapes that were helpful to man. A ring or loop of metal wire is one of the commonest methods of hanging an object such as a lamp or basket from a hook in the ceiling or from a nail in a wall.

By passing one ring through a second, followed by another ring until the required length was reached, the first length of chain was made. The first piece

A very old photograph of early side-welded chain-makers. It is interesting to note the clothes and head-gear that they are wearing.

of chain most probably would not have had its joints welded or forged together to make a complete ring or oval of metal and even today examples of non-welded pieces of chain are still used for purposes where the chain is not required to take a great strain or load.

Before the Second World War the majority of people at home, when they had completed their visit to the lavatory, would 'pull the chain' to flush the toilet. This type of chain is still widely used today for hanging flower baskets and similar tasks. Some of these light chains simply have their ends butted together while some chain-links that need to stand a little more weight are neatly formed into a figure of eight with a second turn of the rod or wire taken around the centre of the 'eight' to lock the link together.

Where strength was required, iron and later steel chain replaced rope for many purposes. Besides having greater strength, metal chain has many advantages over rope. It is able to withstand being flexed continuously, a movement that tends to wear out and unravel a length of rope. When made from good quality wrought iron or good alloy steel, chain is well able to withstand the highly corrosive action of seawater, which eventually rots hemp rope. Many ships have been set adrift or lost their anchors when sharp objects on the sea bottom have cut through their mooring ropes.

Chain is very capable of withstanding a shock load, such as those found when a ship is lying at anchor and is hit by a high wave or gust of wind. Chain is also able to stand the shock of a railway locomotive suddenly pulling away with a train of loosely coupled wagons. Although metal chain stretches a little, especially when it is first subjected to its tensile pull load test, it usually regains some of the expansion later. Rope, on the other hand, will stretch quite a lot

A rare photograph of a three-handled hammer given the nickname a 'Monday hammer' by forge men because, as they told me, 'no one likes Mondays either'. The heads of these hammers weighed anything up to 140lb and five men were required to use them successfully. To the right of the photograph can also be seen a two-handled hammer which had the nickname of a 'johnny hammer'. The heads of these could weigh 60–80lb. In the bottom right-hand corner can just be glimpsed a link of square mooring chain; perhaps this team were working on this.

The Chained Library, Hereford Cathedral

A marvellous quotation is to be found in the exhibition telling the story of the saving, storing and restoration of this unique example of an ancient chained library: 'In the Middle Ages, books were rare and so was honesty . . . a book was worth as much as a farm.'

Early books consisted of manuscripts, which were hand-written with a quill on prepared animal skin (usually sheep or calf) called vellum or parchment. These manuscripts were bound between wooden boards. Before libraries were organised, these treasures were kept in finely carved book-chests. An example of one of these has fortunately been saved and is kept at Hereford. This has three locks, each requiring a separate key; probably each key was held by a different person. One of these early works is the *Hereford Gospels*, which date back to the eighth century. It is one of over 200 medieval manuscripts that are now kept in the Chained Library.

The chaining of books was the most effective way of securing books from the Middle Ages onwards, and Hereford Cathedral's seventeenth-century chained library is the largest to survive complete with all its chains, rods and locks.

The chains securing the books appear to have been made out of square or oblong iron, around ⅛in in section (from a slitting mill?), the size of the links varying, but averaging around 1 $^{15}/_{16}$in long by $^{7}/_{16}$in wide. Many of these links may have been replaced since the library was established in the fifteenth century. The restricting chains were fastened to one of the wooden cover boards of the books by means of a clip or bracket, cut to suit each individual book from a sheet of brass or a staple. Included in the length of chain is a swivel which allows the books to be turned – the books are stored on the shelves with their fore-edges

when put under continuous strain and so will not maintain a load in a set position for very long.

Early Anchors

Early anchors were made of wood but had heavy lead stocks to keep them buried, otherwise the light ropes used by the Greeks and Romans would tend to float and lift the anchor and dislodge its flukes, allowing the boat to drift. Remains of such anchors have been found on the sea bed, but unless the ancient wooden anchor is completely buried to protect and preserve it, the wooden parts will have rotted away leaving only the lead stock intact. These have almost always been found with a square hole through them to take the shank of the anchor. In most cases a bar or bars of lead cross this square hole facing out and not their closed spines as is the normal practice today. The other end of the chain is attached by means of a ring to a bar, which runs along the middle of the shelves and is secured by a lock on the end of the bookshelf. This allows the books to be moved along and set down on the projecting 'reading shelf', situated at waist height. Originally books in libraries were laid flat, which is the most comfortable position for a book but, as collections grew, books had to be stored vertically in the manner which we take for granted today.

In 1590 the whole library was moved to the Lady Chapel, where it was to remain for 250 years. Between 1598 and 1600 a 'three-decker' book-stall system was installed and this survives today. In 1841 the Lady Chapel was required for worship and so the whole contents of the library were removed to the chambers nearby. In November 1855 these chambers were needed for the resident vicar and so once more the books were moved to the archive room in the cathedral; this room was later renamed the transept chamber. It is possible that many of the bookshelves (referred to as 'presses') may have been dismantled and stored in the crypt, while some of them were possibly reassembled in the archive room over the north transept aisle. In 1897 the two-storey Dean Leigh Library was erected and the bookcases were moved to the upper room. In 1929–31 the first great restoration of the chained library took place when the desks, benches and chains were refitted. Around 1,444 books are contained in the Hereford Cathedral Library, making it the largest collection of chained books in the world.

This fascinating story is told in *The Chained Library* by B.F. Streeter, published in London in 1931, which also includes the complete history of the chaining of books in libraries, including private collections.

leading to early investigators speculating that one or more strips of wood were threaded through this hole or holes and lashed together above and below the hole to form the shank of the anchor. This was thought not to be such a good idea as it would weaken the anchor. A French diver, Georges Barnier, solved the problem when diving on an old wreck off Antheor. He found that the lead stock had the remains of its wooden shank still in place. He concluded from his examination that the lead stock was cast on to the shank. The shank with a hole pierced through it was probably up-ended in clay, sand or soil at the position where the stock was required and level with the hole. A mould of the proposed shape of the stock was scooped out on both sides of the shank and the molten lead poured in. Besides filling the mould the lead also passed through the hole and effectively cast the stock on to the shank.

A view across the Dudley Number 2 Canal of Lloyds Proving House, Netherton, showing the 16-ton bow anchor on its horse-drawn wagon, destined for Belfast and the *Titanic* after it had been produced by Noah Hingley a few yards away.

In China there is a mention of the use of both stone and metal anchors as early as 2000 BC, while wooden anchors with lead stocks were said to have been used from early times right up to the nineteenth century.

The lead stocks were very necessary when rope cables were used to keep the flukes of the anchor bedded in the bottom of the sea. When a ship pulls on its iron cable-chain, as a result of wind or current, the flukes of the anchor remain stuck in the bottom because the heavy chain exercises a tangential traction, which is transmitted horizontally on the sea bed. This is known as a 'catenary' and is defined as the curve of an anchor cable as it lies between the anchor on the sea bottom and the ship above. The steeper the curve, the more effect with the catenary. This means that when a pull comes on the anchor it is almost horizontal and tends to bury the flukes of the anchor more firmly into the sea bottom. The good catenary produced by an iron cable-chain also means that a ship rides more easily at her moorings.

Ancient Chains

Proof of the antiquity of chain can be confirmed by mentions in ancient books and documents.

Thucydides, the fifth-century BC Athenian historian of the Peloponnesian Wars, wrote: 'The Plateans, during the siege of their city by the Thebans [429 BC] made use of long iron chains to suspend beams which they dropped so as to break off the heads of battering rams brought up against the city.' We also have Strabo (*Description of the World*), who writes about the history of Alexander the Great (356–323 BC) and tells us that Greek ships at the siege of Tyre were anchored with iron chains so as to prevent the Tyrian divers from cutting the mooring ropes. Another account of the siege of the city of Tyre in 332 BC was written about a hundred years later by Philo of Byzantium (*Veteram Mathematicorum Opera*). He recorded the fact that iron mooring chains were used because Phoenician divers were cutting the mooring ropes of Alexander's fleet during the siege between January and July. The iron anchors, which had light movable stocks, would require iron chain so that they could do their job properly.

Here also are just two of several mentions to be found in the Bible.

> Peter therefore was kept in the prison: but prayer was made earnestly of the Church unto God for him.
> And when Herod was about to bring him forth, the same night Peter was sleeping between two soldiers, bound with two chains: and guards before the door kept the prison.
> And behold, an angel of the Lord stood by him, and a light shined in the cell: and he smote Peter on the side and awoke him saying, Rise up quickly. And his chains fell off from his hands.
> (Acts 12: 5–7. This was *c.* 31 AD).

> And they came to the other side of the sea, into the country of the Gerasenes.
> And when he was come out of the boat, straightway there met him out of the tombs a man with unclean spirit,
> Who had his dwelling in the tombs: and no man could any more bind him, no, not with chain;
> Because that he had been often bound with fetters and chains, and the chains had been rent asunder by him, and the fetters broken in pieces: and no man had strength to tame him.
> (Mark 5: 1–4)

A further notable mention is by Julius Caesar (*De Bello Gallico*, 111, 13). During a battle between Roman ships and the fleet of the Veneti, a tribe from southern Brittany, he compared the performance and the tactics of the ships of both fleets. He makes very interesting observations and important statements from which we can learn quite a lot. One statement relevant to this chapter is to the effect that the Veneti anchors were secured fast by iron chains instead of cables or ropes (‘*Ancorae pro funibus ferreis catenis revinctae*’). Honor Frost in her excellent article ‘From Rope to Chain’ (*The Mariner’s Mirror*, 1963) says that ‘From this statement the Veneti were credited with the invention of the anchor chain.’

This tribe, who traded with people on the Wessex coast, eventually settled there and built their own hill forts. In 1881, during investigations of one of these hill forts east of Bere Regis known as Bulbury Camp, an iron anchor – complete with a length of iron chain – was discovered. It is referred to as the Bulbury anchor. When found the links of the chain were corroded together around the stock end of the shank. It remained in this condition in the Dorset County Museum until 1967 when an extensive programme of cleaning and conservation was carried out in the Dorset County Laboratory. The chain, once it had been cleaned up and separated, was found to be made up of 113 oval links. This was attached to the stock end of the anchor by means of a large ring. Another similarly sized ring was inserted three links away from the anchor ring; this was possibly used for stowing or ‘catting’ the anchor when the ship was under way. The overall length of the chain and rings was 21ft 4in.

The Bulbury anchor was probably made some time in the first forty years of the first century AD. Similar anchors of the same period have since been found in London on the River Thames embankment and in Pompeii.

Early Defence Chains

Lengths of chain, some of them quite large, were used several hundred years ago as a defence against raiding or invading ships. Some locations had a succession of defence chains. The first recorded chain to span the Medway between Upnor and Gillingham was set in place in 1583. M. Oppenheim in his *A History of the Administration of The Royal Navy* (1896) refers to information in old documents to the effect that, ‘In October 1583, the work was nearly completed, it had been tedious and cumbersome, but now stretched over the river in “good order yt dothe require many lyghters for the bearynge of it which are in hand”.’ The lighters or barges referred to would be moored at intervals across the river to support the defence chain either just above or just below the surface of the water.

Another defence chain is mentioned by Commander Crofton in his book *The Dutch in the Medway, June 9th to 13th, 1687*. He provides us with a little extra information: ‘. . . the exact locality is not known but it stretched from

Hoo Marsh to Gillingham, the width of the river being 700yd.' Commander Crofton points out that Pepys's reference to the chain being 6½in in circumference (that is $2^{1}/_{16}$in in diameter) is clearly a mistake because the total weight of the chain is stated in the naval papers in Chancery Lane as 14 tons 6cwt. A chain of this size would only span a width of river of around 150yd. It is suggested that the 6½in measurement possibly relates to the overall length of the chain-link. This would give the diameter of the chain (from the size of the bar that the links were made from) as being about 1⅛in.

'In the reign of Henry VIII,' writes W.G. Gates in his *History of Portsmouth* (1900), the entrance to Portsmouth harbour was protected by a 'myghtie chayne of yron'. This defence chain was produced in 1522 and Gates tells us that several links were still buried in the mud and could be seen at low tide close to the Round Tower. James E. Bradney, in *Chains by a Chain Maker* (1949), adds to this information by telling us that it was supplied at a cost of £40. It was buoyed across the mouth of Portsmouth harbour using three barges and came into use in 1545. About a century later it was replaced by another chain, the older one being left in the mud. Again some of the links of the chain could be seen at low water and, around 1929, one of the links was recovered and measured. The overall dimensions recorded were length 3ft 8in and width 1ft 2in. It is not stated which defence chain the link came from, so it could be either the sixteenth- or seventeenth-century one.

It is interesting to note, however, that these sizes compare closely with the square-link mooring chain that was produced by various chain firms well into the twentieth century. Examples of these are preserved at the Plymouth Dockyard Naval Museum.

Another defence chain was used in the north-east of England on the River Tyne. Napoleon threatened to invade England in 1803 using flat-bottomed boats and it was decided to defend the mouth of the Tyne in case there was an attempt to burn shipping that was moored there. Ambrose Crowley & Co. of Swalwell, County Durham, whose works were located about 5 miles south-west of Newcastle-upon-Tyne, manufactured a strong iron chain that was laid across the bed of the river and attached on each side to capstans. At a given signal, the capstans would raise the chain in order to obstruct the passage of fireships. The system was actually put to good use on one occasion when a ship called the *Popplewells Pink* caught fire in the entrance to the harbour and threatened to set fire to other ships nearby. The chain was raised and caught the stricken vessel, which by this time was 'blazing, fore and aft', and held it until it had burnt out.

Another well-documented historic defence chain was sited across the Hudson River in America. It was placed in position in April 1778 close to

A photograph of a number of preserved links of the river defence chain that was put in place near West Point on the Hudson River in New York State in 1778. It is very similar to the large square mooring chain then being made in England. It was fastened to large log floats and used to stop British ships passing up the river. It was used for four years, being taken up in the winter when the river froze over. *(Reproduced by kind permission of Michael J. McAfee, West Point Museum)*

what is now the US Military Academy at West Point to prevent British men-of-war sailing through and taking advantage of the waterway system and the nearby great lakes during the Revolutionary War. While carrying out early research into chains I wrote to Michael J. McAfee, the curator at the West Point Museum, requesting information regarding the defence chains used. He was very helpful and supplied me with a great deal of information together with permission to reproduce the photograph of a large number of links that had been saved and which are proudly displayed along with other historical ironwork in the grounds of the West Point Academy.

In December 1777 General Washington wrote to General Putnam in New York saying how important it was to maintain water communication and possession of the Hudson River in that area. Early in February 1778 Colonel Hughes, Deputy Quartermaster-General of the Continental Army, was despatched to the Stirling Iron Works of Noble, Townsend & Company at Warwick, New York. He arranged for the necessary chain-links, swivels, anchors, clevises and the other assorted iron fixtures that were required, to be forged so as to form a defensive 500ft chain across the Hudson River close to West Point. The chain was to be made out of 2¼in square iron, the links being 2ft long with a swivel fitted every 100ft. Colonel Hughes contracted to pay '440 pounds (continental money)' for every ton weight of chain and accessories delivered.

Sixty men were employed making the chain and the forges were told to work around the clock because of the urgency of the project. It was delivered in ten-link sections in March 1778, and it was buoyed across the river using fourteen to sixteen log floats, each composed of four logs 40–50ft long, assembled like a raft with 12ft logs as cross spars. The chain was stapled to the floats. For four years the chain was taken out of the water each winter and replaced as soon as the ice had gone. The ice formed an effective barrier during the winter months. No British ship ever challenged the chain and it was taken out of the water for the last time in the winter of 1782 after the Battle of Yorktown.

Development of the Modern Chain Industry

Although chain in various forms has therefore been made and used by man for thousands of years it is recorded that in about 1808 an Irish blacksmith by the name of Robert Flinn, who had his forge in Bell Street, North Shields, was probably the first man to produce iron cable-chain for the anchoring and mooring of ships. Ship owners and operators had been looking for a substitute for hemp cable for some time because it was getting more and more difficult, owing to the various wars that were constantly raging on the continent, to obtain the hemp to supplement the British-grown supplies to make hemp mooring cable.

Marine ropes are chiefly manufactured from manila hemp. The base fibres, the cellulose cells which support the stems of tall upright plants, are obtained from the phloem of jute, flax and hemp. Hemp, one of the principal fibres used, may grow to heights of 10–15ft. The fibre is obtained by cutting down the plant near the root and stripping off the leaves. The layers towards the centre of the stem are found to be fine in texture and white in colour while the outer layers are dull brown and of a coarse texture.

Slave Chains from the Past

A reminder of the hard but skilled work carried out by Black Country women in their backyard chain-shops came to light recently when an email was passed on to me by Stephen Howard from the Black Country Living Museum at Dudley.

It was a request from Lalou Meltzer, head of research and interpretation in the Social History Division of the Iziko Museums of Cape Town, South Africa. It was a plea for help as they had been 'searching high and low for someone interested in this field'. They had been trying to identify, and date, a number of slave chains that they have in their collection. Many of these with closing and locking mechanisms were probably made in the lock factories of Walsall while the chains and swivels were probably fitted to them by the women chain-makers of the Cradley Heath district.

The recent combination of the Willenhall Lock Museum and the Black Country Living Museum means that experts from Willenhall organised by Sheila Hennings and experts on the chain trade of the Black Country, organised by Stephen, were able to supply valuable help and information to the Museum of Cape Town to identify the type and give some idea of the date that these historic slave chains were made. On examining the illustrations it was possible to see that all but one of the examples had chain fitted to it that had been made by hand; the other one had electrically butt-welded steel chain, which had its links joined on the side. It was also possible to see that some were leg irons (oval shape), while some were for the wrists and another set was designed to be used around the neck to keep a group of four slaves together.

The area around the town of Bridport in Dorset was found to have the soil and climate suitable for growing hemp and flax, and the town soon became known as the main producer in Britain of twine, string, cordage and rope. As early as the thirteenth century Bridport was granted a charter to supply the king's ships with cordage. King John sent orders in 1211 for ships' cables. However, the industry declined in the eighteenth century as a result of competition from the naval ropeyards at Woolwich, Deptford, Plymouth and Portsmouth. Another problem in the area was the silting up of Bridport harbour.

In 1793 it was estimated that there were 1,800 rope- and net-makers in Bridport and another 7,000 people employed in the industry in the surrounding countryside. In the early nineteenth century iron cable-chains gradually replaced ropes for anchoring ships and this exacerbated the decline of the heavy rope-making industry in Dorset. The last ropeyard closed there

Slavery was abolished in the British Empire, mostly because of the hard work of William Wilberforce MP, at midnight on 31 July 1834. Having said that, slave chains were still being made because, although on that date 800,000 slaves in British possessions were rejoicing at gaining their freedom, many more slaves around the world continued to wear chains to restrict their movements.

A man was interviewed in Cradley Heath in 1934, a hundred years after Wilberforce's hard work bore fruit, who recalled making slave chains in his backyard forge, as did his father before him and many neighbours who lived around him. He went on to say that similar chains were still being made in the district for use in the USA on cotton plantations, but these were 'breast chains'. These were worn across the chest, and attached to wagons loaded with cotton, to enable them to be hauled about the plantations by humans.

At the height of the production of slave chains in the district, the old Collins's Bakery, on the corner of Foxoak Street and Newtown Lane in Cradley Heath, still standing today, and about 40yd away from the Parish Church of St Luke on the 'Four Ways', served as a storage warehouse where 80–100 tons of chains at a time were gathered awaiting shipment overseas.

When I started researching and recording the local hand-made chain trade in the district in the late 1960s, many women chain-makers could well remember slave chains being made, especially in the cluster of women's chain-shops in Plant Street, Old Hill, which were only demolished in the 1970s.

in the early twentieth century. In the layout of Bridport town today the long narrow plots of land that were once occupied by the many rope-walks can still be made out.

Up to the early nineteenth century, when the first iron cable-chain was produced, Royal Navy ships of the line usually carried ten or eleven hemp cables. According to the tonnage of the ship, some of these were quite large, some of the largest being 25in in circumference or around 8in in diameter. It is interesting to note that the equivalent size of iron cable-chain required to carry out the same task would use 2¼in diameter metal. In *Chain Cables and Chains* (1885) Thomas W. Traill made a comparison of the price difference between the two types of cable and stated, 'When hemp could be procured at a moderate price, such a cable [hemp] would have cost about 20 per cent more than its equivalent iron cable.' One of the reasons for experimenting with the use of iron cable as a substitute for hemp cable was that the majority of the latter had to be imported and its price at the beginning of the nineteenth century was soaring.

The Royal Navy, hearing good reports about the 'new' iron cable-chain, decided to carry out trials. Admiral Sir Henry Stanhope was given the task of putting iron chains through various tests on HMS *Namur*. With several captains also on board, including Samuel Brown, they carried out various operations in a strong easterly wind with a strong flood tide running, and everyone expressed their admiration for the efficiency of the iron cables.

In 1812 the commander of the transport *Aid*, equipped with iron cables, satisfactorily rode out gales while other vessels close by that were equipped with hemp had their cables parted. His report was so favourable that the Navy Office issued orders for three more Navy transports, the *Assistance*, the *Portsmouth* and the *Chatham*, to be fitted with one iron cable-chain each.

As confidence grew in the use of iron cable-chains by ships of the Royal Navy, they were specified for use in greater numbers. It was decided to install machines for the testing of iron cables in the naval yards. The first one, which had the distinction of being the first machine of its type to be installed in a government establishment, was put in at Woolwich in 1833. Other machines soon followed at Plymouth and Portsmouth. The navy yards on the Medway had to wait until the 1850s to have their testing machines installed.

At first merchant ship owners, who quickly changed from hemp to iron cables when they became available, found themselves having to pay higher insurance premiums to the underwriters because the superiority of iron over hemp cables was not generally recognised. This handicap ended in 1836 when the extra premium was dropped because it was accepted by the insurers that ships' cable-chains were made to a high standard of quality and were more reliable.

In 1831 the naval authorities gave instructions that ships were to be supplied with iron cable-chain on a larger scale. Larger vessels were equipped with four lengths of iron cable, while sloops were allowed to carry three lengths and cutters two. At the same time the number of hemp cables carried was reduced. From the time that the Navy had first experimented with iron cables it therefore took twenty-one years for the Admiralty to accept that the number of iron cable-chains carried should equal the number of anchors on the ship. As confidence grew in favour of iron cables the number of hemp cables carried was further reduced.

The Location of Chain-Makers in Great Britain

In the early nineteenth century chain-makers could be found in many counties of Great Britain where wrought iron was available. In these early

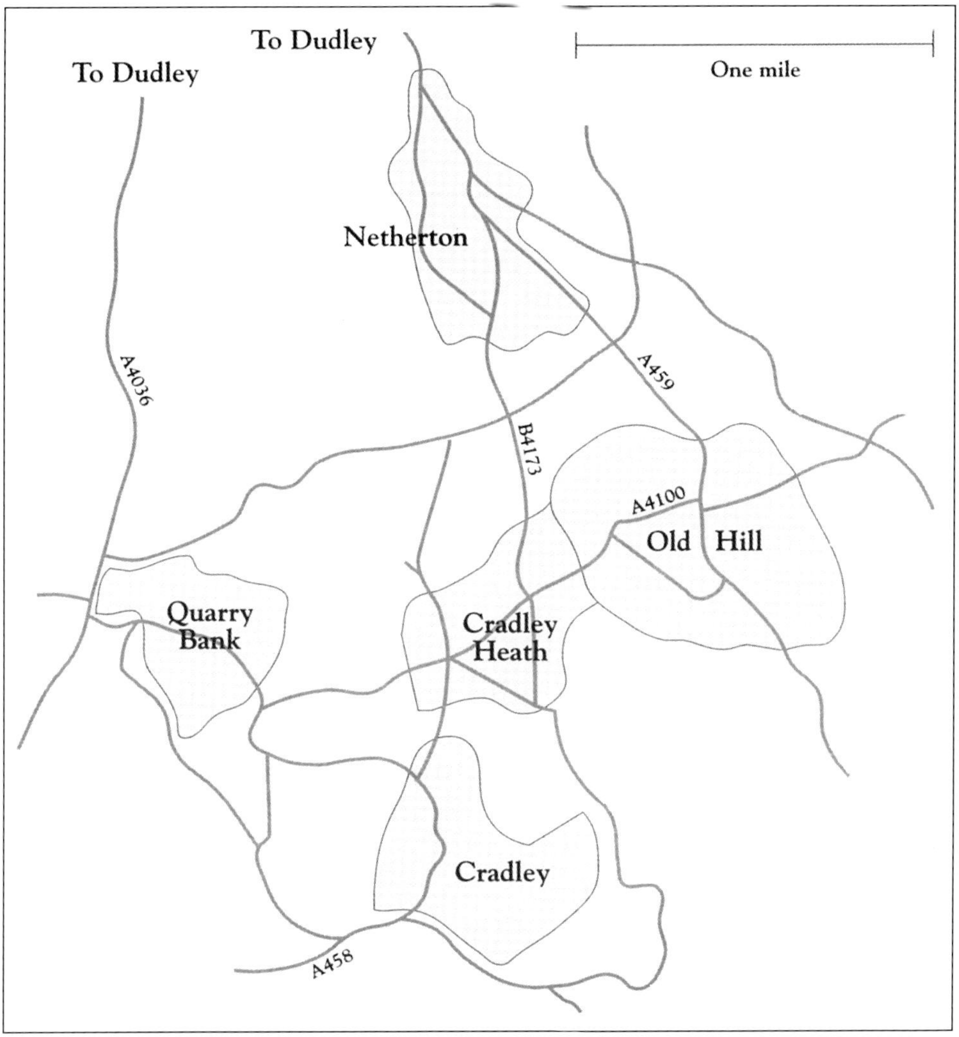

Chain-making townships in the Black Country.

days they were mainly employed making agricultural chain for use on farms. By the early twentieth century the majority were to be found in the Midland counties or, to be more precise, South Staffordshire and North Worcestershire plus the part of Worcestershire around Dudley that was isolated in Staffordshire. This area forms what is generally accepted and known as the Black Country and from the re-organisation of local government and counties that took effect from 1 April 1974 became part of the West Midland County.

Sydney Allen found when carrying out his research into labour relations and trade unionism in the wrought-iron chain-making industry of the Black Country (Birmingham University, 1981) that 'From the mid-nineteenth century, Cradley Heath was fast becoming the geographical centre of the chain-making industry. . . . The organisations representing both male and female chain workers had their headquarters and offices in that area.'

Professor R.H. Tawney carried out some excellent research in an earlier era which he then presented in his book *Minimum Rates in the Chain-making Industry* (1914). For this publication he collected details of wages, hours worked, and ages and sex of the workers in the chain-making district just after the Chain Trade Board had fixed minimum wages. Making good use of the last census returns available to him, he was able to compare the total number of chain-makers in England and Wales with the number to be found in what he called 'the chain-making townships'. These he recorded as being Cradley, Cradley Heath, Old Hill, Quarry Bank and Netherton. A glance at a map of the area shows that all these 'townships' fit into an area measuring

Square mooring chain on display at Chatham Dockyard on Navy Day, 30 May 1999. It is probably made from 3–4in square iron and the standard specification calls for '3ft long clear' in the centre of the link. This type of chain was produced by several of the large chain-works in the Black Country. *(Ron Moss)*

roughly 2½ miles wide by 3 miles long. In 1911 the census figures tell us that the total number of chain-makers in England and Wales totalled 7,323, out of whom no fewer than 6,550 resided in the counties of Staffordshire (4,073) and Worcestershire (2,477). The Cradley Heath Ward accounted for almost 2,000 of the Staffordshire total. Other figures illustrated the concentration of the chain industry in the area. Out of a total of 938 chain workshops (small chain-shops producing small-chain, as different to chain-works) that appear on the Home Office list of 1911, 918 are in the Cradley Heath area.

I have in my possession a list of the addresses of chain-shops and chain-works in England, Scotland and Wales emanating from the Office of Trade Boards, Whitehall Gardens, London, dated December 1934. It runs into seventeen pages, giving names and addresses of chain-shops and chain-making firms in such scattered places as Rochdale, Liverpool, Glasgow, Coatbridge, Carlisle, Bristol, Durham, Manchester, Pontypridd, Chester and Shifnal. I thought that it would be interesting to carry out a survey to discover whether in 1934 the concentration was still contained in the same area. The total of names on the lists came to 224, out of which the chain-making town-ships cited by Tawney accounted for 182. A breakdown of the survey showed that Cradley Heath had 68 while neighbouring Old Hill, 1 mile away, accounted for 72 (a total of 140 between them); Quarry Bank had 17 and Netherton 15, while Cradley had 20.

Nearby Walsall, just outside the Black Country, which has been famous for several hundred years for its leather craft skills connected with horse transport, had a supporting chain-making industry. Although a lot of harness and agricultural chain was produced in the Black Country for Walsall companies, the town still had six chain-making firms listed in 1934.

In his book *Chain Cables and Chains* (1885) Thomas Traill gives us a list of cable-chain-makers at that date, who were producing the large studded variety of chain, which was normally made by fairly large firms because extra operations and machines were required. The list covering Wales, Scotland and England lists a total of twenty-eight firms, out of which no fewer than nineteen are situated in the Black Country.

An interesting point to make here is that electrically welded steel small-chain, which was first produced in England (Cradley Heath) in 1903, was by the time of the 1934 list being turned out literally by the mile by several firms, and after a shaky start was now a reliable product. Many small family chain-shops would have been put out of business by this time by the mass production of small-chain, thereby reducing a little the total number of chain-shops recorded.

Electrically welded steel and alloy-steel cable-chain is still produced in the Black Country area by several firms while different firms produce the smaller electrically welded steel chain, with both men and women making use of automatic machines today. Quite a degree of skill is still required to set up and tool these machines. The last producer of hand-made wrought-iron chain ceased production in the winter of 1976 and the early months of 1977, one of the reasons being that the bars of wrought iron required for its manufacture were no longer available, although one or two small firms produced hand-made chain for a little longer using low-carbon mild steel.

A historic photograph taken at the Henry Wood Chain Works at Saltney, near Chester, when King George V paid the company a visit. Side-welded chain-links that have just come off the bending machine can be seen in the right-hand corner of the picture. The king is accompanied by the works' director.

Chapter 2

The Hand-Made Chain of the Black Country

The most suitable metal to use in the manufacture of chain that has to withstand long terms of restraining a load or being able to take a sudden snatch load is wrought or puddled iron. It is tough, has excellent ductile qualities (that is, it can be worked and shaped easily and smoothly and maintains its shape without cracking or breaking), and it can be joined to other wrought iron using a blacksmith's fire-weld, which unites the metal with a natural join and maintains its original qualities. In the early nineteenth century, when the region began making the larger cable-chain used for anchoring ships, its excellent anti-corrosive qualities added to its suitability for use at sea.

Flat Winding Chain

The history of the development of flat chain, known in the Black Country as 'rattle chain', can be traced back to the 1770s when John Wilkinson (the famous ironmaster), while at Bersham Ironworks, found that, as his iron castings became larger and heavier, something stronger and more reliable than hemp rope was required to lift them and move them around his works. He carried out experiments with iron chains that he had manufactured for moving his cylinders and cannon about. These he had made from cast iron rather than the wrought iron that eventually became the standard and most suitable metal used for the making of chain. It would be interesting to know how he manufactured this early chain because cast iron is very brittle and is not able to withstand a shock load, an essential requirement for chain, and it cannot be forged or fire-welded. He had obviously produced a reasonable chain by 1777 because Matthew Boulton, of Boulton & Watt fame, observed

Hancock's Chain

The Royal Society for the Encouragement of Arts, Manufactures and Commerce was founded in 1754 to encourage the development of industry in England. For several years this society offered a premium of 50 guineas to anyone who could develop a metal rope or chain that would 'answer the purpose' of a hemp rope.

While carrying out research into early chain-making in the Birmingham Reference Library I came across this extraordinary account of the development of a metal rope that was used by several engineering firms who later sent in glowing recommendations for the product way back in 1795. The inventor was a William Hancock, who is described in the book *Birmingham Inventors and Inventions* by R.B. Prosser (1881) as 'a Birmingham workman', who first of all decided to use cold-drawn wire for the material to make the chain-links. We know and appreciate today that iron and steel wire (or any metal really) that is cold-drawn through dies immediately has any fault in the product highlighted because, as the metal is drawn through the dies and comes to a foreign body or a weakness, it breaks. As Prosser points out, 'If the inventor had stopped short before the bending operation he might have been handed down to posterity as the originator of wire rope, but this does not seem to have occurred to him.'

From the description and on examination of the illustration, the chain was made out of many strands of drawn, wrought-iron wire, making up a diameter of around ⅜in, and formed into a 'figure of eight' link, joined together. The joins in the links do not appear to have been welded. A William Johnson of Bradley tells us in his testimonial that it weighed 'about three pounds per yard'. A similar type of chain is still made today and used for toilet flushing chain and dog leads and other light uses, but it is made from single-strand wire only.

In the 1796 edition of the *Transactions of the Society for the Encouragement of Arts, Manufactures and Commerce* several glowing testimonials were published from engineers and manufacturers who made good use of 'Hancock's chain'. William Johnson wrote in December 1795 to say that he had made good use of one of Hancock's chains in his 'foundery' (*sic*) for 'five or six years past', for loading large castings etc. He went on to say that the iron wire of which it was made was about ⅜in diameter, and occasionally lifted 2 or 3 tons.

in a letter: 'Mr J. Wilkinson's cast-iron chains are now much superior in metal and workmanship to what used to be made.'

The next person to enter the story is Gilbert Gilpin, who was chief clerk to Wilkinson at the Bersham Ironworks, near Wrexham, and also the Brymbo Ironworks during the period 1786–96. He noticed that chains were being used

The chain was apparently made for Hancock by a William Bingley, who had a Plated Wire Works in London and used the chain for drawing large wire, a good test of strength for the chain. He said that the chain was far stronger and would last much longer than the hemp rope that he previously used for the purpose.

312 MECHANICKS.

We have had ſome of thoſe Chains made from Engliſh and Foreign Iron, but they have ſometimes failed, through the iron being faulty.

The only iron to be depended upon, is thick wire, as the drawing of it detects any fault in the quality. Chains made from this wire would come into more general uſe inſtead of ropes, if it were not for the ſcarcity as well as high price of this kind of iron.

We have had a Chain from Hancock a few weeks ſince, ſeventy-one yards long, bare three-eighths wire, weight two hundred and ſixteen pounds, or about three pounds per yard; will work two tons. If the obſtacles before mentioned were not in the way, we ſhould have thoſe Chains in more general uſe than they are; but this objection ſhould not deprive the claimant of the merit due to his invention.

I am, SIR,

Your moſt obedient ſervant,

WILLIAM JOHNSON.

Bradley,
Dec. 2, 1795.

Mr. MORE. *Mr.*

Mr. WILLIAM HANCOCK'*s Metal Rope or Chain.*

Detail and description of the $\frac{3}{8}$in chain that was made by William Hancock from drawn iron wire in 1795. *(Birmingham Central Library)*

for winding up the pit shafts in the coal mines in the area around Wrexham 'with mixed results'. He left Wilkinson's service in 1796 and spent a short period of time at the Soho Works of Boulton & Watt near Birmingham. In the early weeks of 1797 he moved from Birmingham to South Wales where he took a great interest in the development of Henry Cort's method of making wrought iron by the puddling process. He was also involved as a partner in a marble quarry and the mining of lead ore.

By the middle of 1799 Gilpin was back in Shropshire working for Botfield & Son at the Old Park Ironworks, where he was able to put to good use the knowledge that he had gained regarding Cort's method of puddling iron. As the shafts of collieries became deeper, mining engineers earnestly sought a reliable substitute for hemp ropes. So, in his spare time, Gilpin experimented using chain for winding up the shafts of local collieries. He continued with his experiments after moving to the Stirchley Furnaces of the Botfield Company near Shifnal. He was awarded a silver medal and 30 guineas in 1805 for his work on perfecting iron chains and grooved guides for use in pit winding gear. This enabled the chains to remain at right angles during winding.

Botfields began to notice that Gilpin appeared to be devoting more and more time to his chains than to the work that he was employed to do for them. In 1807 he decided to leave Botfields and move to Coalport and set up his own works for the manufacture and supply of best 'horse-nail' iron and chains for use in the pits and on cranes. Gilpin's chains proved to be a suitable substitute for ropes and so replaced them in many uses.

When iron chains were first used in collieries they were in the form of single lengths. It was soon realised that if a chain broke in service lives would be at risk and an improvement was sought. To encourage development Joseph Reynolds of Ketley offered a prize of £50 to anyone who could come up with a safer method of using the chains.

Into the story now comes a Benjamin Edge, who had been making chain at Coalport since around the year 1800. He would have been aware of Gilpin's experiments in using chain for winding cages up the shafts of collieries, as both of them worked and lived in the same town. In the interests of safety Edge had the idea of putting three pieces of chain made from rectangular iron alongside each other. The chain consisted of alternate long and short links, oblong in shape. He fitted a block of wood (usually oak) through the three longer links at the start of each piece, which physically joined them together to form a flat belt of chains around 5–6in wide. This belt was attached to the cage at one end, the other end being wound on to a drum that had iron struts or guides fitted to its sides to enable the belt to be accommodated, one turn on top of another. This meant that the depth of shaft in which it could be used was limited. The date of this improvement is recorded as 1810.

This type of winding chain was soon nicknamed 'rattle chain' because of the noise that it made when winding was in progress. To keep the belt lubricated and to try to cut down some of the noise made it was liberally coated with a very thick oil with the consistency of gas-tar (or pitch).

Ted Attwood is seen here scarfing a chain-link at the Noah Bloomer Chain Works in Quarry Bank in 1975. His tommy hammer is not the normal type working between two wood stumps but has the hammer pivoted in a bracket fitted on the bickon. It is still worked by a treadle action. I once heard this type of hammer referred to as a 'portable'. I can imagine a smith taking the set-up with him to join chains in his customer's yard.

Rattle chain was gradually replaced by wire rope, as this was developed and adopted. The earliest recorded date I have found for the first use of wire rope is a reference in the *Journal of the Iron and Steel Institute*, 1903. This states that

This view shows one of the early stages in the manufacture of a hand-made chain-link. The cut length of metal bar is heated, then cranked, and then hammered into the U-shape, seen here, before being put back into the fire. Some of the finished stud chain-links can be seen hanging in the background. The chain-maker is Sam Bloomer, working in the Noah Bloomer (no relation) yard in Quarry Bank, in 1975. He is making $^3/_4$in diameter cable-chain. *(Ron Moss)*

wire rope was invented and first used by Albert of Clausthal in 1834. The *National Encyclopaedia* (*c.* 1890) gives a slightly earlier date, stating that 'Ropes of twisted iron wire were first used in the silver mines of the Harz mountains in Germany in 1831.'

Gilbert Gilpin died at Dawley in 1827 but his pit winding chains continued to be manufactured at Dawley until 1910 by a chain firm established by a Charles Merrington. Merrington served an apprenticeship in chain-making at Benjamin Edge's works at Coalport and, on completing this in 1820, left to set up his own chain-making firm in Southall Road, Dawley.

Edge moved to Shifnal and established a fairly large chain-works there, naming it Coalport Works to commemorate the original site. The Chain Makers' and Strikers' Silver silver jubilee booklet of 1914 contains a photograph of a group of chain-makers at Edge & Sons, Shifnal, with examples of flat winding chain arranged in front of them.

Rattle chain was used in some coal mines in the Black Country possibly up to the period 1915–20, though I have been unable to find a chain-maker who can recall seeing any flat chain being made. Jones's trade directory of 1865 lists several 'flat chain makers' in the Cradley Heath section, and the makers of different types of chain are identified.

Round Bar Chain

To allow chain to be flexible and its links to work smoothly together the optimum form of metal that is required and laid down in chain specifications is a truly round bar. To produce this shape, hot wrought-iron billets are passed through sets of rollers until the size that is required is reached. Today this is taken for granted and rolling mills swiftly turn out miles of rounds, bars and rods to customers' requirements. It is hard to believe that this process is recorded as being introduced only just over 220 years ago.

Henry Cort is generally credited with the introduction of grooved rollers in 1783. He experimented at the Funtley Ironworks (owned by the Earl of Southampton) near Fareham in Hampshire until he perfected the process and was able to patent it. Before Cort's invention any object that was required to finish in a round section had to be obtained as a square or oblong shape, heated to a red heat, and hammered into a round form before final shaping could take place.

As a guide to the time saved by the introduction of the rolling process, one set of figures produced stated that before Cort's invention it took twelve hours to turn one ton of square bar iron into round iron by heating and hammering while the same amount could be converted by hot rolling in three-quarters of an hour. The diameter of the bars was not given in this example.

In theory, then, any chain produced before 1783 either had to be made from square or oblong iron or, if round was required, the bars had to be forged into round shape before the link could be formed.

It is also worth remembering that, when these dates are quoted, everything does not change overnight on that precise date. A good example of this is contained in the description by Traill in his *Chain Cables and Chains*, covering the introduction of the first iron cable-chain.

In the section 'Historical Notes On Chain Cables' he relates the story of how, before 1808, ships' cables, which are used to lower and raise the anchors, were made from hemp. At the beginning of the nineteenth century, partly due to various wars, hemp was becoming scarce and the cost of importing it from such places as Turkey, Russia, India and the Philippines was rising. As usually happens, necessity was the mother of invention and a reliable substitute was sought to replace hemp. The story goes that, from quite an early age, Robert Flinn was trained in the art of blacksmithing by his uncle, Thomas Black. He established a workshop in Bell Street, North Shields, where he soon became an expert in his trade and became famous for making high-quality harpoons used by whale fishermen. He obtained a supply of rectangular iron bars from Wales, which he soon proceeded to work into rounds on his anvil using his hand hammer. From this round iron he then made the first cable-chain in Great Britain of modern times, the year being 1808. So we can see that, although Henry Cort had pioneered the production of round iron by rolling mill using grooved rollers in 1783, twenty-five years later at the other end of England a blacksmith was producing round iron by the time-consuming method of using a hammer and an anvil.

This first iron cable-chain was made for use on the 221-ton vessel the *Ann and Isabella*. Its links were very similar to the short-link chain manufactured today, maybe slightly longer but of course they would not be fitted with a stud or stay-pin, as fitted to cable-chain today. We have to wait until 1813 when Thomas Brunton is credited with the introduction of this. The 'stud' was introduced to prevent the entanglement or knotting up of anchor chain when the anchor on a ship was dropped or 'let go'.

The first cable-chain was a great success. On one occasion, during a severe winter when the *Ann and Isabella* had several ships made fast to her on the Tyne, she happened to be the only one that was fitted with an iron cable. The other ships were still anchored with hemp cables. Their cables were sliced through by a flood of water containing large pieces of floating ice but they were held fast and saved by the iron cable of the *Ann and Isabella*.

I mentioned above 'in Great Britain' because it was brought to my notice by John Stonehouse of Burton-on-Trent that an earlier date is quoted for the continent. *History of the Royal Navy* edited by Peter Kemp (1969) describes how, on 21 August 1801, Lord Nelson decided to strike a blow in the enemy's back yard by carrying out a raid on Boulogne to attack Bonaparte's invasion barges. The idea was to cut their mooring ropes so that they would drift away. The raid failed because the enemy ships were moored with the 'new-fangled chain cables instead of the more usual rope'.

Here Michael Bradney carries out the final operation when adding another link to a twisted tram-brake chain. To ensure a smooth pull-up on the brake coil casting, after the chain-link is fire-welded it is placed in the U-shaped tool on the anvil and, while still held with the tongs and hot, a bar is inserted in the link and it is twisted through 90 degrees.

The news of the success of the iron cable soon spread and other firms in Great Britain began making it. However, the Black Country had to wait until 1820 before the first iron cable-chain was manufactured in the area by Noah Hingley, who at that time had a chain-works in Newtown, Cradley Heath.

Trade Unions

For hundreds of years tradesmen have banded together to protect their trades, skills, rights and their living. Even the masters and the men together formed themselves into craft guilds in the early days and these were much respected. In the eighteenth century tradesmen working by the day, who were known as 'journeymen', combined together for protection against the people who employed them. The employers were not very pleased with the loyalty and strength of the people in these 'combinations' and by means of an Act of Parliament they had many of these associations, which had been organised in several trades, banned. There were a great number of trades that were not affected by this Act and they had many members who were highly skilled workers, many of whom had served a recognised apprenticeship and if an employer decided to dismiss them they were not easy to replace. Some combinations or trade societies were formed under the guise of 'friendly societies' who looked after their members with regard to illness, unemployment, death and even strike pay, although this latter category was probably not legal under the Friendly Societies Act of 1783.

The wars with France at the end of the eighteenth century were used as an excuse to ban these associations as a possible source of revolutionary ideas. The Combination Act was passed in 1799 and this banned any contracts or negotiations that were made that might affect the wages earned or the hours worked. It also prevented the hindering of any person or persons from employing whomsoever he, she, or they should think proper to employ. This last point is usually of the utmost importance to the satisfactory working of guilds and trade unions.

The 1788 Combination Act not only applied to workers, but to associations of employers as well, carrying a maximum punishment of three months' imprisonment. Despite this legislation, and amendments, combinations quietly continued. With improvements in the state of the country it was suggested in the House of Commons that a Select Committee be appointed to look into industry and the working of the Combination Acts in the early 1820s. This committee recommended a complete repeal of the Combination Acts and this took place in 1824 and 1825.

From 1825 the way was open for workers, mostly skilled men, to form themselves into trades unions. One setback to trade unionism, which is

The house in the middle with the centre doorway was once the residence of a chainmaster and is typical of the abodes they kept in the mid- to late nineteenth century. Obviously windows have been modified and extensions have been added, and the houses on each side were built later. Many works' owners lived in this area of Lawrence Lane, conveniently situated midway between Cradley Heath and Old Hill.

recorded in history books throughout the world, was the trial of the 'Tolpuddle Martyrs', as they became known, in March 1834. At the end of the trial they were sentenced to the maximum of seven years' transportation to Australia, not for forming a union but for the oath that they were innocently ordered to take at their initiation ceremony, which the government regarded as possibly having revolutionary content. There was such an outcry against this sentence that within two years they were all brought back to England. This strong-arm tactic by the government affected recruitment to the unions and some employers took advantage of the situation by making workmen sign a paper promising that they would not join a union and made this a condition of employment.

The chain-making industry has a long, varied and chequered history relating to its trades unions. Anyone wishing to learn about its history is recommended to peruse the thesis of my great friend, Sydney Allen, a copy of which is retained in the University of Birmingham. Syd recalls that, to his knowledge, the first union connected with the chain trade was the Chain-

Unity Villa, for many years the headquarters of the Chain Makers' Union, situated in Sydney Road, Cradley Heath.

makers' Benefit Society, which was established in Gateshead in 1841. Two more early unions were the Chain & Tracemakers' Society founded in Cradley Heath in 1844 and the Cradley Heath Chainmakers' Co-operative Industrial and Provident Society, also founded in Cradley Heath in 1854 by James Gill.

On Sunday 10 April 1859 representatives of the northern unions came south to meet the South Staffordshire chain-makers. Some of the local union men waited on the Sunday evening at Dudley station until the last train, but the men from the north had carried on to Netherton station, ten miles from Birmingham, and on stepping down from the train found themselves in the heart of the Black Country. From there, it is reported in their journal, they walked to Cradley Heath, a distance of 2 or 3 miles, where they were heartily received by Thomas Homer, the district secretary of the union who soon found them quarters at the inn kept by Benjamin Billingham (known locally as 'Benny Fiddler' because he played the fiddle to entertain his customers); this was the Bell Inn, just off the Five Ways, Cradley Heath, in Scolding Green Road, now renamed St Anne's Road. Billingham (1811–95) had left the chain trade, but was most respected by the chain-makers. In one of the severest chain strikes that ever took place in Staffordshire, Billingham had advanced the men £700 to aid them in their struggle; to their credit, every last penny was repaid.

On Monday 18 April a general meeting was due to be held by the chain-makers at the New Pool dam, Cradley Heath (this dam held back the water for the famous Cradley Forge), to which the northern representatives were invited. The journal went on to say that 'The stormy aspect of the day obliged us to adjourn to Mr Billingham's large room.'

The representatives from the north visited several local chain establishments during their stay as their journal recounts:

> On Tuesday we took farewell of our friends in Dudley and were accompanied back on the road to Cradley Heath by Mr Wise, whose kindness, and those of the friends who act with him we will never cease to remember.
>
> We then visited Spinners End [between Old Hill and Cradley Heath], near to the Five Ways, Cradley Heath, where we saw numbers of women and girls making 'American Swimmers', as they are called, or more properly 'traces, cow bands, small twist link etc.'
>
> This sight will not be easily effaced from our recollection. For while we boast in England of our Christianity, there are things done, which if the sun were made to shine upon them, would appal the heart.
>
> We propose to write a special paper upon this subject, and cannot touch further upon these unpleasant and degrading scenes; but if God spares us with health and strength, we will use both voice and pen to endeavour to effect their abolition.
>
> We may, however, correct a mistake which many North Countrymen fall into, by saying that, throughout the whole of Staffordshire and Worcestershire, probably not more than half a dozen women are employed in making hawser or cable chains; but too many work at 'swimmers'!

Thomas Sitch founded the United Chain-makers' and Chainstrikers' Association of Saltney, Pontypridd and Staffordshire in Chester (Saltney) on 6 July 1889. The name was changed to Chain Makers' and Strikers' Association (CSA) in 1899. Its head office later moved down to Cradley Heath, in Unity Villa, Sydney Road. At one time the CSA boasted a membership of 2,000 but by 1977 this had dropped to 140, with most of them retired. Mr Albert Head was its most efficient secretary for many years and when he took office the association had a credit balance of just £5. When in 1977 it was decided to disband the CSA the assets were £32,000. Sydney

Allen's father, Frederick Allen, was president of the union in 1944–68. He also held the post of press correspondent throughout 1918–68 and had the useful ability to compile accurate records of the minutes of the meetings using shorthand.

Between the last decade of the eighteenth century and the first decade of the twentieth, the wages of chain-makers are recorded as improving considerably. In the larger works where the 'big chain' was made, the chain-makers obviously benefited from the development of their unions. During the same period, the wages and conditions of the small chain-makers, many of whom were women, but also men and women outworkers, were gradually improved as well because they too organised themselves. Lots of sterling work was carried out by such people as Lady Dilke, Julia Varley, Ada Heather Bigg and Mary Macarthur together with other members of either the Women's Trade Union League, the Anti-Sweating League or the National Federation of Women Workers, who led the women in their fight to be paid the minimum wage that the 1910 Trade Boards enquiry had recommended and the employers refused to pay.

The Minimum Wage and the Chain Industry

Early attempts at wage regulation in King George III's reign were repealed in the reign of King George IV around twenty-five years later. A few workers on public contracts were afforded a little protection by 'Fair Wages' resolutions in February 1891 and March 1909 but apart from these it was left to workers to bargain with their employers until the introduction of the Trade Board Act of 1909. The chain manufacturing industry was one of the first four industries that were scheduled under this Act to try to establish a minimum wage.

Information supplied by the Registrar-General tells us that in 1911, out of a total of 7,323 known chain-makers in England and Wales, 6,550 were employed in the Black Country area that sits on top of the 10yd coal seam located in North Worcestershire and South Staffordshire. One of the obvious reasons for this is because of the availability of small coal in the area that can readily be turned into small coke, known locally as 'breeze', in local breeze ovens that were to be seen in batches of two or more near the mouth of the many hundreds of coal pits in the area. Various sizes of breeze were found to be the ideal fuel for the clean hot fires required in the hundreds of chain-makers' hearths in the chain-making districts.

Of the 6,550 chain-makers to be found in the Black Country, Staffordshire had 4,073 with 3,038 residing in Rowley Regis UDC, the Cradley Heath Ward accounting for 1,990. In Worcestershire 2,477 were recorded, with 890 of these in the Country Borough of Dudley.

Examples of price lists and contribution cards that were issued by the Chain Makers' & Strikers' Association. These cards covered most of the various types of chain that were made and were issued when prices altered.

There were a couple of dozen or so reasonably sized chain-making firms making the smaller size chain (made from iron bar usually no larger than 5⁄16in or 3⁄8in in diameter) in Cradley Heath employing from twelve to thirty chain-makers each. On obtaining an order from a merchant they would retain so much of the order themselves to keep their own workers busy and farm out a proportion of the work, complete with bundles of iron of the correct size, to 'middlemen' who again would use their own makers to produce part of the order. If the order was required fairly quickly or it was of a decent size, the work would also then be offered out to small family chain-makers who had 'brewhouse chain-shops' or 'domestic workshops' to the rear of their houses, 'across the blue paved yard', in which many of the family worked, the mother and father, with the children lending a hand when they returned from school. By the time that they left school at the age of thirteen the children were fully skilled craftsmen (or craftswomen).

The chain-making industry in Cradley Heath is described by R.H. Tawney in his *Studies in the Minimum Wage* (1914) as using the same methods in the twentieth century as had been employed in the eighteenth. In fact the tools used were little changed from those used by smiths in the fourteenth century. Although the larger chain, that is that over 3⁄8in in diameter, was made in factories after around 1820 because of the machinery and processes required to make it efficiently, the smaller chain below that size was still mainly produced in the small chain-shops or brewhouse chain-shops to be found at the rear of, or attached to, the chain-makers' dwellings. In 1910 around 3,500 workers made chain in small shops at home, probably twice as many as the number of workers making chain inside factories. What was more, around two-thirds of the home workers were women. Many of them had once been employed making nails and had been displaced from that trade by the machine-made nails that were being produced in Birmingham from around 1820 onwards. They had found a use for their skills of working iron in the fire in their hearths at home. The skilled men made the larger chain in the factories with many of them being employed in the making of cable-chain for anchoring ships. Many of the orders for this chain were for the Royal Navy and the Admiralty specified that this chain must be made on the contractor's premises. The specification called for a high-quality product and it had to be proved on a test bed to the Lloyds Breaking & Tensile Strain List to carry the load required for that size of chain; a certificate was then issued accordingly.

With all these women coming into the chain trade the male chain-makers working on the smaller sizes were getting quite worried that the women would take over their jobs. The men tried to limit the women by trying to set a legal limit on the hours that they could work and also to try to prohibit them from working on chains exceeding ¼in in diameter. They also suggested that women should not work on a tommy-hammer; this again would prevent them from making the larger sizes of chain. Their excuse was that 'women were not strong enough to weld the larger sizes without exertion'. The commissioners who were appointed to look into the working of the Factory & Workshops Acts in 1876 immediately refused to grant this request.

Figures taken from census returns show a dramatic increase in the number of women coming into the chain trade in the counties of Staffordshire and Worcestershire. In 1861, 19.7 per cent of all the chain-makers coming into the trade were women. In 1881 this had risen to 25.4 per cent and by 1911 the number was 32.1 per cent. Fortunately the number of children coming into the trade had fallen because of the Education Acts and it was suggested that the age at which children might be employed should be raised to fourteen.

By 1888 the competition from female labour seems to have faded somewhat and most of the attention of the Commissioners appears to have shifted to the middlemen, the evils of the domestic chain-shops, long working hours and low pay. One suggestion was that parliament should fix a minimum rate of wages while the president of the Chain-makers' Society wanted a maximum working day for men of eight hours. Another suggestion was that co-operative factories should be established with the capital being advanced by the state. By purchasing the iron and then selling the chain for the best price in the market, the middlemen would be cut out. The scheme was approved by the Midland Trades' Federation and several small factories were established, but all had faded away within two years.

The proposal to establish minimum rates of payment was rejected by the committee of 1888–90. The mere fact that wages were so low meant that workers could not organise and form a union. When the chain-makers thought that they would have to pay 3*d* a week to the union they compared this to the cost of a loaf of bread. Because wages were so low they were underfed and were living on 'bread and a drop of tea', and as one report said 'you cannot make chain all day on bread and tea'.

One of the most important events in the history of the chain trade was the formation in 1905 of a women chain-makers' organisation under the title of the Cradley Heath & District Hammered and Country Chain-Makers' Association, which in 1907 became known as the Hammered Chain Branch of the National Federation of Women Workers. The formation of this union publicised the plight of the poorly paid chain-makers and led to the scheduling of 'hand-hammered and dollied or tommied chain-making' as one of the industries to which the Trade Boards Act of 1909 was to apply.

A parliamentary Select Committee on Home-Work was appointed in 1908 which reported in favour of establishing Trade Boards in four industries. Unfortunately when the Trade Boards Bill was introduced the chain industry was not in the list. It was eventually included but only after the very hard work, skill and energy of Mary Macarthur. Cradley Heath chain-makers, both women and men, have never forgotten the work of this fine lady. Since the trade was largely concentrated in a small, compact area it became the first one to be dealt with by the Trade Board, out of the four that were designated to receive attention. And so it became the first industry to have minimum wage legislation applied to it since the repeal of the Spitalfields Act of 1824.

Mary Macarthur and the 1910 'Lock-Out'

Mary Reid Macarthur was born in Glasgow on 13 August 1880. Her parents ran a successful drapery business and were able to live a comfortable life from the trade that they had worked hard to build up. Her father was proud to be regarded as a leading Conservative in the area and, as Mary matured, he encouraged her to develop the same political views. Mary helped her parents in their drapery shop and at the age of twenty she was invited to attend a meeting of fellow shop assistants and write a feature on what went on for a local newspaper. At this meeting Mary was converted to socialism after listening to the militant speaker who addressed the assistants.

That meeting was to change Mary's life completely. Not long afterwards she moved to London and became associated with the women's trades unions. In 1903 she succeeded Lady Dilke as secretary of the Women's Trade Union League. Lady Dilke had for many years championed the crusade against the exploitation of the working woman. She also founded the National Federation of Women Workers in 1906, becoming its first president. Around the same time she paid her first visit to Cradley Heath to make a speech in the Empire Theatre to women workers and on this visit it is recorded that she was shocked at the poverty she saw and the infant mortality rate that she found in the area.

In 1906 Charles Dilke had proposed the setting up of a Trade Board which would look into fixing minimum pay rates for the hammered and dollied or tommied section of the chain trade. This trade had been scheduled as a 'sweated trade' under the Trade Boards Act. After several years of hard work a bill was introduced in March 1909 to establish a Wages Board. This would contain representatives of both employers and workers and was passed through the Lords in the autumn and on 3 January 1910 received the royal assent.

The board, with the Right Hon. Winston S. Churchill at its head, was made up of three appointed members including a barrister, six chain-masters

Mary Macarthur acknowledging the ovation of the surrounding crowd of women chain-makers, many in caps, and their children during the 1910 chain strike in Cradley Heath. *(Edwin Beech Imperial Studio, Cradley Heath)*

from the Cradley Heath area, and six people representing the workers. The members of the board were as follows: three appointed members, namely, W.B. Yates (barrister), Thomas Smith, Mona Wilson; six employers, chosen at meetings of employers held on 6 December 1909, namely Noah Bloomer, John Fellows, G.H. Green, Lashford Griffin, Caleb Woodhouse, Joseph Woodhouse; six workers' representatives, also chosen at meetings on 6 December 1909, William Bate, William Cooper, Josiah Griffiths, Charles Homer, Mary Macarthur, Thomas Sitch. The Board of Trade also appointed W.B. Yates as chairman of the Trade Board, and J.A. Heaton as secretary.

Under the regulations the workers were allowed to have 'skilled advisors' to help them. Several women from the Women's Trade Union League came up from London, one of them of course being Mary Macarthur who immediately stepped in to help. She stated in her notes that when the Chain-making Board first met she found, as was natural from the conditions of their trade, that the chain-makers were 'ignorant, inarticulate and inexperienced' at negotiating. She also wrote at the time that,

> . . . his [Tom Sitch's union] members received good wages; some of them can make 15 shillings for a day's work of six hours. The unorganised men and women [not members of the Chain Makers' Union], mostly working at home, receive hardly enough to provide them with shelter and cheap coal. A husband and wife working together may count upon one pound a week.

Most women workers were recorded as earning 4–5 shillings a week.

At the meetings 'the employers for their part seemed hard and unhelpful'. The bartering at the meetings began by each side offering rates knowing full well that the other side would not accept them. Statements were made to the effect that if undue rises were promised the chain trade might suffer from foreign competition or the workers would be replaced by machinery. Both Mary's tolerance and patience were tried as time and time again the meetings held to set the new wage rates ended in deadlock. Finally, in May 1910, the new minimum rates were fixed. Where the employer provided the fuel and the tools in addition to the iron and place to make the chain the minimum time-rate was to be 2½*d* an hour. In all other cases (which meant the chain-makers working at home and providing their own tools and fuel) the minimum time-rate was to be 3⅓*d* an hour; a piece-work price of 7*s* 6*d* per hundredweight was also set.

This meant a wage increase of between 60 and 150 per cent for the women chain-makers and the employers said that they would not pay the new rates until compelled to. They also found a loophole in the agreement. The Act allowed the workers to contract out from the new rates for six months and there was also a delay of three months before the published rates came into force. The employers took advantage of the workers' ignorance or poor education by circulating documents among them which requested exemption and demanded their signatures. Not fully understanding the significance of the documents, the majority of the workers signed away their chance of an increase in wages for almost nine months. In the next few weeks some of the employers had their workers build up huge stocks of chain, even working overtime, hoping that by the time that the new wage rates came into force they could lay off their workers and blame their unemployment on the Trade Boards Act.

Mary Macarthur had foreseen this happening and at a meeting organised by the Women's Trade Union League and the Anti-Sweating League she proposed to mobilise the good employers and they agreed to pay the new rates, provided that under the Act they would be safeguarded against undercutting from the other chain-masters.

A mass meeting attended by about 400 women was called at Graingers Lane Sunday School (this building was only demolished a few years ago) and the women agreed to come out and stay out until Mary told them otherwise. One old lady told me that Mary came into her works because they were too frightened to come out. When she told them, 'Out you go and join your fellow workers', they looked sheepishly at their gaffer who, seeing the determined look on Mary's face, said, 'Yowed better goo then.'

One of the local newspapers of the time, the *Midland Evening News*, reported that 'Almost 200 women are locked out of their workplaces with around 500 more without work'. The 500 mentioned would have been outworkers who worked at home but depended on the owners of the chain firms to supply them with metal and orders. The women cheered Mary at the Graingers Lane meeting when she announced that, from the money that had been donated into their strike fund by well-wishers, they would be paid 4*s* a week for the duration of the strike. It is believed that this was the first industrial action to be publicised by the new cinematograph medium and money started to flow in to the union funds from all over the country. George Cadbury, the chocolate manufacturer of Bournville, promised to pay £10 into the funds every week for the duration of the strike.

The women left the meeting in great spirits and marched through the streets of Cradley Heath singing rousing songs. Standing on one of the street corners, fascinated by the goings on, was none other than the famous writer John Galsworthy. He wrote his account of the parades and included it in his book *The Inn of Tranquillity*, entitling the relevant chapter 'The Procession'. He also donated £10 to the women's funds.

Numerous meetings of the women chain-makers were held in the district, many in Graingers Lane Sunday School and some on the 'spoil-bank' of the Whitehall Colliery, Lomey Town, close to where the Workers' Institute was later built.

The strike, or lock-out, went on for around ten weeks and lasted from 21 August until 22 October 1910 and eventually, thanks to the determination of Mary Macarthur, the women got their promised wage rate as determined by the Trade Board.

From figures provided by women who took part in the strike and who appeared in the BBC television programme *Nothing to Lose* (broadcast in about 1970), some idea of the wage increases that the women gained by taking part in the strike was recorded. In figures later published, it was stated that the average wage that the women took home before the lock-out was 11*s* 3*d* a week, although from other records that I have seen many were lucky to take home 5*s* a week, while after the strike the average was said to be 14*s* 6*d* a week.

Women in the Chain Industry

Women formed a substantial part of the Black Country chain-making industry. Many of them specialised in making the smaller sizes of chain from not much larger than watch chain to around $^{11}/_{32}$in in diameter, which of course was the size of the bar that the chain was made from.

The census returns of 1841 tell us that 44 women were recorded as having the trade of making chains in Staffordshire and Worcestershire. This total had risen to 2,103 by the census of 1911. The period of the First World War, when the Army required a vast amount of chain to harness the many horses and equip the numerous wagons that were used, meant that everyone who could make chain was working flat out with plenty of overtime being worked. With the return to more peaceful conditions, the greater use of motor vehicles, the availability of cleaner, better-paid employment in other trades and the development of electrically welded machine-made small-chain, the number of small-chain makers plummeted.

Having said that, the manufacture of small-chain once again increased to satisfy the requirements of the Second World War, with many domestic workers in their backyard 'brewhouse' chain-shops only finally laying down their hammers in the 1950s. To my knowledge the last female chain-maker, Mrs Lucy Woodhall, laid down her hammer and tongs in December 1973 having made chain for over sixty years. I was very fortunate to watch her, and photograph her, at her hearth, making small, twisted chain. She retired from one of the oldest chain-making firms in Cradley Heath, Samuel Woodhouse & Sons, in 1973, probably the last woman making chain by hand in the country, maybe even the world. Ironically Samuel Woodhouse was the first firm in the country to experiment with, and make, electrically welded chain under licence in 1903.

Lucy Woodhall told me that she left school on her thirteenth birthday, which fell on a Friday, and began her apprenticeship the following Monday in November 1912. One of the conditions of the two-year apprenticeship was that she first had to pass a medical examination. This was carried out in the boss's kitchen by a visiting local doctor. She proudly told me that she passed this with flying colours. She commenced her training by pumping the bellows to keep the fires in the hearths of her fellow workers in the chain-shop hot and glowing.

As an occasional relief to this job she was allowed to 'go on the block'. This sometimes referred to the iron or steel block into which were located and

Lucy Woodhall, probably the last female chain-maker in the Black Country, maybe even the world, shutting a link of number 2 twisted chain ($^9/_{32}$in diameter) at the Eagle Chain-Works of Samuel Woodhouse & Sons, Cradley Heath, in September 1973. She retired three months later aged 73, after making chain for over sixty years. *(Ron Moss)*

wedged the various tools necessary to make small-chain, or sometimes to the 'swedge' itself, which was one of the tools set in the block on which the bending of the metal rod was carried out. She was shown, and then told to practise, the operation of 'turning a link'. This was the second operation in making a link of small-chain. Women usually worked 'from or off the bar'; that is, they would thrust the iron rod or bar into the fire in the hearth, making sure to heat a sufficient amount of metal to make or form the chain-link. They would then butt the hot end of the rod up against the stop of the pre-set adjustable gauge, laying the rod on the top of the 'hardy' (the chisel-shaped cutter), and then give the rod a hearty blow with the hammer, but not quite hard enough to sever it from the rest of the rod. While the piece of work was still attached to the rod, they would then fashion a U-shaped hook on the end of the rod using the swedge; this was generally known as 'turning a link'. The half-finished link, still held in the grip of the tongs, was heated to working heat again, taken out of the fire, threaded through the last link made, and the other side of the link turned on the bickon (also referred to as the 'bicken' or 'bick-iron').

She was later shown the skilled art of 'shutting a link'. After the iron link had been brought up to welding heat in the fire (the correct temperature of the link being judged by eye alone), it needed just a few accurate blows with the hammer to 'fire-weld' the two ends together or 'shut the link'.

As a lot of the chain made by women was 'country work' (for use on the farm) there then followed an extra operation carried out while the link was still hot. This was known as 'twisting the link' which meant that half of the chain-link was twisted 90 degrees from the other half to allow the chain to lie neatly flat (resembling the shoulder epaulette on a guardsman's uniform). This operation was carried out by locating the welded link in the 'twister', which was a P-shaped tool fitted in the bickon, putting a long-handled hooked piece of metal known as a 'dog' around the hinged part of the tongs that held the link, and deftly twisting it. With practice, all the twists in the length of chain would be identical, allowing the chain to lie flat. This was all part of the female chain-maker's acquired skill.

Lucy's training was punctuated by other menial duties such as sweeping out the chain-shop and on Saturdays by cleaning out the lavatories. In 1912 when she first started her job she would begin work at 7.00 a.m. and continue until 7.00 p.m., Monday to Friday; on Saturday her hours were 7.00 a.m. until 2.00 p.m. Her wages were 4*s* a week. Before leaving on Saturday the work floors had to be swept up and always left clean and tidy.

After six months, as she had made satisfactory progress, her weekly wage was increased to 5*s* 6*d* per week. After twelve months she was sufficiently skilled to be able to move on to 'stint work'. A stint consisted of a specified amount of work that she was supposed to produce per day. If she completed this before her normal finishing time she had a choice of either going home early or carrying on working. The extra production made in that time was weighed each Saturday and would be priced at the 'piecework rate'. Lucy told me that this sometimes amounted to as much as an extra 2*s* 6*d* a week, 'a lot of money in those days', she said. This was very useful to help support her family because her father, owing to a health problem which was a legacy from the Boer War, was not able to work regularly.

An excellent example of a women's chain-shop of the type that produced hundreds of yards of small hand-made chain. As you can see the women are quite young. On view in front of the chimneys on the right-hand side of the shop are the handles that they had to use to pump the bellows to supply blast to their fires. This shop was operated originally by Harry Stevens in Oak Street, Old Hill. When he died his son, Mark, ran it, but when he died in 1958 it closed for business.

Training for the Trade

I have never seen a formal, legal indentured apprenticeship agreement for a girl chain-maker but I have seen several agreements for boys. The earliest one that I have seen was a photocopy of an indenture from the year 1867. This was an agreement between a Samuel Dunn and Edge & Sons, of Coalport, Salop (James Edge is hand-written above the firm's printed title). This firm was famous for producing 'flat' or 'rattle chain' and also produced 'hand-dollied' chain up to at least 1¼in in diameter.

The indenture is one of the horizontal-oblong pre-printed certificates that were used for a number of trades starting with the flowery lettering telling us that 'This Indenture Witnesseth That Samuel Dunn doth put himself apprentice to Edge & Sons . . . from the First of July, one thousand, eight hundred and sixty seven until the first of July, one thousand eight hundred and seventy three unto the full End and Term of Service Years'. It then goes on to set down the conditions of his apprenticeship, such as, 'He shall not commit fornication nor contract matrimony within the said term. He shall not play at Cards or Dice Tables or any other unlawful Games . . . He shall neither buy or sell and shall not haunt Taverns. . . . '

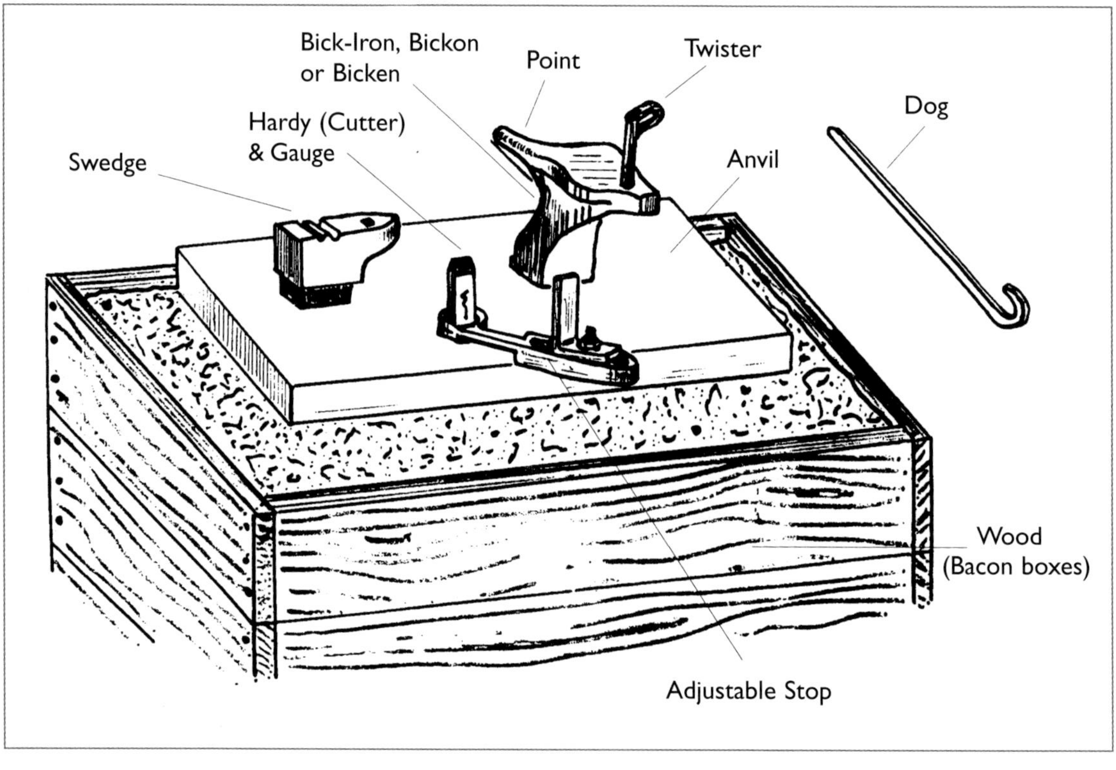

Women's tools. *(Ron Moss)*

It then proceeds to specify what Dunn would be paid while training: '. . . shall receive one shilling per day for the first 12 months and advance two pence per day each following year until the full term of years are expired'. It then goes on to say that the said apprentice will be trained in the art of chain-making. The number of days to be worked per week is not given but would probably be six. This means that at the end of his training period his wages could be 12*s* per week. If correct, this appears to be quite a good wage for the year 1873.

Another indenture that I have seen, covering the later period 1872–9, actually specified a term of seven years and two months, though this was from a different district. This particular agreement was between William Henry Simon Tate of Cradley and the famous chain firm of Jones & Lloyd of Cradley and is dated 2 August 1872. This sheet is a vertical oblong version but contains the same conditions as the previous one mentioned in that the apprentice shall not play cards or dice and also adds that he 'shall not haunt taverns nor ale houses' – but does not mention matrimony.

It continues that, in consideration of his faithful services, they will instruct him in their art, trade or calling of 'Nail & Chain Manufacturers'. It then goes into great detail on the wages that they will pay him. They promise to pay him from the time that he starts work up to 25 September 1872 the sum of 4*s* per week, then from 25 September 1872 up to the same day of September 1873 the sum of 5*s* per week, and so on until 'from the 25th day of September 1878 until the end of the term the sum of eleven shillings per week of lawful money'. The final wage figures are thus comparable with the earlier Coalport indenture even though that was dated six years earlier. In the last but one paragraph the father, William Tate, has to sign to agree that he will find the apprentice sufficient meat, drink, clothes, washing and lodging, and all other necessaries during the said term.

A very thoughtful 'memorandum' is handwritten on the reverse of the indenture saying that in the case of the death of either of the masters, Joseph Jones and Lewis Lloyd, the indenture will be binding on the apprentice and the successor or successors of either of the masters.

I wondered if there were any deductions made from the apprentices for the supply of air-blast for the hearths. Most men and women chain-makers while working for a master around that date had the cost of providing the blast for their hearths deducted from their wages at the end of the week. An example of this is mentioned in the article 'Nails and Chains' by the Revd Harold Rylett, vicar of Dudley, in *The English Illustrated Magazine* of 1889–90. This tells us of a man who was making ½in diameter chain, 378 links to the hundredweight. It said that if he worked 'hard and long', a strong man might make 6cwt in a week and if he be paid the current list price for his labours, he would earn 24*s*, out of which he would have to pay his blower 4*s*. It is also recorded that, out of the meagre few shillings that the women chain-makers earned, a portion would be deducted for blast.

It was quite a feather in the cap of the United Chain Makers' and Strikers' Association when, by negotiating with the employers, their union executives were able to arrange terms of settlement, without having to call their members out on strike, to put an end to the practice of charging the chain-makers for providing the blast. An announcement in the 14th Report and Balance Sheet of the union for the period ending 26 June 1897 stated that 'This was a grievous burden for them to bear, and we resolved to rid the trade forever of this load, and so place all workmen and employers on a level.' It then went on to say that the ending of the deduction for blast charges was equivalent to a 10 per cent advance in wages, and was a grand testimony to the growing influence of organisation. It did not forget to thank the officers of the federation for their help in obtaining this important settlement.

At the first conference of the Saltney, Pontypridd & Staffordshire Association, which later became the United Chain Makers' and Strikers' Association, held on 22 August 1892, proposals were made regarding apprentices in the chain-making industry: 'That this Association will only allow one apprentice to the chain-trade for every 10 qualified chain-makers in each factory, and that no other apprentices be allowed to start, when one batch of apprentices are serving their term.' It was also proposed 'That the term of apprenticeship shall be three years and that the Condition of Prices, as allowance for learning, shall be 10 per cent, for the first year, 5 per cent, for the second year, and full price for the next year.'

This 'Condition of Prices' referred to was the 'Price of Chain' lists for piecework that were negotiated between the workers and the employers, at different periods, printed, and issued by the union. These were often referred to as the '4 shilling list' or the '5 shilling list'. For example, the price of all sizes of chain on the list was related to the price quoted for one hundredweight of ½in diameter chain. If the price quoted was 5*s* per hundredweight then the list was referred to by everyone as 'the 5 shilling list'. Therefore the conditions laid out above meant that the master or factory owner would pay the apprentice the list price of the size of the chain that he was working on, deducting 10 or 5 per cent for himself to cover the cost of tuition, training, wasted metal and fuel. This was a clever way of making sure that the apprentice was always being paid the current rate for the chain he was making rather than legally binding rates that were specified in the indentures, which might lag behind if prices rose. The employer was likewise covered if prices or demand fell. Also at the same first conference it was agreed that the general secretary should contact other societies to see if they too can 'take up the apprentice question for the whole of the chain trade'.

The other type of apprenticeship was the informal one in which fathers brought their sons into the trade and taught them all the skills that they had mastered over many years. This was the only way in which some of the older chain-makers would pass on their knowledge and so preserve the high-class skills that they had developed. All the little tricks of the trade that they had learnt from experience, sometimes over half a century of hard graft, would never be found in any book. They would willingly be passed on from father to son, or even grandfather to grandson. One only has to refer to lists of employees at the large firms such as Noah Hingley to see the same family name appearing again and again. Sometimes whole 'fires' (hearths) would be manned by members of the same family. Sometimes the members of a gang would have different names but upon investigation it would emerge that they were uncles and nephews or brothers-in-law or related in some way. It is not uncommon to find whole families being connected with the large firms without a break, even for a century.

Among the outworkers there was a great deal of 'patrimony'; in fact, one woman that I spoke to told me that it was traditional in families that all the sons and daughters had to learn the art of chain-making. Her mother taught the members of her family and she told me that the reason that she was never taught was because her mother died before her turn came.

Children in Chain-Shops

Several old photographs showing the interior of small chain-shops have come to light during research showing women at work, and they also clearly show small children either standing by their parents and relations in the chain-shops or actually sitting on the boxes in which the working block and tools are set. An inspector from the present Health & Safety at Work Executive paying a visit to the shop would certainly be shocked to find young children in such a dangerous environment. Obviously a lot of women had to work and earn money just to help their husbands so as to provide a living wage to enable them to raise their families and pay the rent. If some of their children were below school attendance age, then the only place that their mothers could keep an eye on them was in the chain-shop when they went to make chain.

It is a well-known fact that in the days before electric blowers were introduced, and the women had to generate the air-blast that was necessary to blow the fires in their hearths by pumping large horse-shoe bellows, they would place their babies in a basket on top of the bellows. The occasional half

The Crowley Industrial Empire

Many early industrial families, especially those who were non-conformists, tended to keep their family name alive by each generation using the father's Christian name for every first-born son. We find this method being used by the Crowley family and also the Darbys of Coalbrookdale, just to give two examples.

The Crowley family is first recorded in Rowley in the Black Country when Ambrose Crowley was described as a nailor with a small-holding. He was born around 1615 and he worked hard to feed and clothe his family. His probate inventory dated 30 October 1686 (which can be seen in Worcester Record Office) tells us that when he died he left movable goods valued at £24. This included his forge, farm tools and two cows.

Ambrose Crowley II was born at Rowley in about 1635 and in his father's will he was left '12 pence in silver, and 6 shillings and 8 pence, to be shared between his wife, his children and himself'. He is recorded as living in Stourbridge in 1657 having the trade of 'a nailor'. By 1682 he was living in a town house in Main Street, Stourbridge, and had established a steel furnace, out of town, at Tiled House, Bromley. Robert Plot mentioned this in his *Natural History of Staffordshire* (1686). Crowley would probably have been taking advantage of the local Amblecote clay, which can withstand the terrific heat required for the cementation process of making steel which was current at that time. Marie Rowlands in her book *Masters & Men* (1975) mentioned a steel furnace that was being managed in 1712 by James, a son of Ambrose Crowley II born in 1683.

In 1682–3 it is recorded that Crowley II refused a knighthood, saying that, being a Quaker, 'I disclaim all right to arms and gentility.' In 1688 he granted by indenture the Friends Meeting House and burial ground in Queens Road/Wollaston Street (now part of the Stourbridge Ring Road), which is still in use today. He died in Stourbridge in 1721, aged 86. His properties, which included a steelworks and an iron forge, were valued at £1,181 3*s* 8*d*.

Ambrose Crowley III was sent from Stourbridge in 1663 at the age of 15 as an apprentice to a London merchant. In 1671, two years out of his apprenticeship, he is recorded as setting up a warehouse in Thames Street, London. He continued the family connection with the nail industry, supplying the Navy and ship-building industry with the many nails and metal parts necessary at that time for building and maintaining wooden ships.

dozen pumps on the handle connected to the bellows would rock the baby to sleep, helped of course by the warmth given out by the fire in the hearth. It appears that the babies learned to sleep through the noise of the hammering

In 1683, at the age of 26, Ambrose Crowley III located his business in Sunderland, not according to tradition at that time near to the source of the fuel and raw materials, but to take advantage of the water transport then available from the north. He found it much quicker and cheaper to send his finished products by sea from Sunderland and Newcastle than overland from Stourbridge. This came in useful later on when the firm started supplying large chain and anchors to the Navy. Colliers were leaving the north-east with loads of coal bound for the south; these voyages were regular and reliable and Crowley was able to take advantage of this.

In 1690 Ambrose Crowley III transferred his ironworks from Sunderland to Swalwell and, although the firm continued to manufacture in the Midlands, the main centre of the business shifted to the north. This developed into the largest single industrial organisation in the land at that time. Mr Bailee, in his book *Impartial History of the Town and County of Newcastle upon Tyne and its Vicinity* (1801), described the works as follows: 'Here in huge furnaces are forged anchors of vast size, chains of prodigious magnitude for our ships of war, East Indiamen and all Europe.' Ambrose Crowley III received a knighthood in 1707, an honour that was purely routine as he was then one of the two Sheriffs of London and Middlesex. He died in 1713 at the age of 55, and it is recorded that he was worth over £100,000. He is buried in Mitcham Parish Church and in that church there can be seen a bust of Sir Ambrose and Lady Mary Crowley.

After being in the Crowley family for nearly 170 years, all stock and plant from the Northern Works (Swalwell & Winlaton Mill) was sold on 10 February 1863 to Paw & Fawcus of North Shields for the sum of £780. This firm continued to make cable-chains until 1878.

The last mention of the Crowley family in the north-east occurred in a newspaper report in the *Gateshead & Newcastle Evening World* of 14 August 1929 when it reported that 'the buildings of the Old Crowley Steel Works' were being demolished for road widening. Over the entrance to the moulding shop was the inscription 'Ambrose Crowley, anno 1713'.

The tradition of numbering was carried on by the son of Ambrose III's daughter, Mary, when he called his son Ambrose Crowley IV. He was born in 1718 and died in 1754.

that went on all around them. This practice must have been carried on from quite early times, so much so that the metal pivot that formed the simple universal joint enabling the operator to pump the bellows from a variety of

Two women chain-makers with bedraggled hair and urden-bag aprons working in the group of chain-shops in Plant Street, Reddal Hill, between Old Hill and Cradley Heath. The woman on the right is making twisted chain.

positions while standing in the working area in front of the hearth became universally known as the 'rock'. It is even recorded in an inventory of 'all the goods and chattels and credits of one William Rock, late of Rowley Kings [Rowley Regis] deceased, taken and appraised, the 10th day of November 1740'. This lists the contents of his nail-shop as including 'One pair of Bellows, Rock and one Stock, One Steady, One Hammer, One Bore'.

A descendant of the man who established a family firm in 1850 in Quarry Bank, and one of its present directors, told me a story that his father had passed on to him regarding the time when they employed both women and men making chain in their works. One of the women who made chain on the end hearth in the main workshop was quite clearly pregnant. She was a typical hard-working Black Country woman, one who produced excellent chain and 'kept herself to herself'. One day it was noted that her hearth was 'cold' and quiet, and she did not make an appearance. She came in the next day carrying a well wrapped up new-born baby which she carefully placed in a box close to the warmth of her hearth and proceeded to put in a good day's work making chain, punctuated by the feeding of her baby as and when necessary. He also told me that around that time his father spent a whole day each week delivering iron rods to his outworkers. An illustration by Tom Hill that accompanied the article 'Nails and Chains' by the Revd Harold Rylett showed not only a baby resting on top of the bellows but another one suspended in a type of chair by a rope from the roof timber truss behind the woman who is making chain. I presume that occasionally she turned around and gave the 'swing' a push.

Throughout my research into the chain industry I have found instances of women chain-makers having their babies and being absent from their hearths for shorter and shorter periods of time. The shortest time noted to date concerned a Mrs Greenfield. I found out from her son that she made small diameter chains in her brewhouse chain-shop that was situated across the yard to the rear of her home. The day that she had her baby she made chain from 6.00 a.m. until 6.00 p.m., crossed the yard, went into her home, and with the help of the local midwife gave birth to her baby. The midwife then tightly bound her up with flannel, and she returned to her forge across the yard at 10.00 p.m. and continued her chain-making. She passed away in 1969 at the age of 74.

Her son told me that he helped his mother by carrying a half hundredweight of iron bars at a time from the Old Hill Ironworks, which was about 1½ miles away in Powke Lane, Old Hill. He can recall her making one hundredweight of chains a week for which she was paid the sum of 6*s*.

Children would also, after school hours, help their parents by cutting off the rods and part bending them for a little pocket money so that they would soon become quite proficient at working the iron at an early age. It is not surprising that many of them followed their parents into the chain-making trade. This also happened in other local trades. A lock-maker at Willenhall once told me that he had 'pottered about' in local workshops making parts for locks in his spare time when not at school, so much so that when he left school at the age of eleven he was a fully skilled lock-maker, and had no difficulty in obtaining a job immediately.

Children in Workshops

A wealth of information dealing with child labour is to be found in a collection of books that have never been reprinted and are only available to researchers on the shelves of our largest national libraries. These are sometimes called Blue Books. They contain fascinating facts that were collected by various government inspectors and officers and appear as minutes of evidence taken before government or parliamentary inquiries, committees and commissions on various subjects. The reports and conclusions founded upon these inquiries give us quite an accurate insight into the working conditions of children in the formative years of the industrial revolution in the British Isles.

The very early proposals for legislation to control hours and conditions of work were aimed mostly at children. As many of the early industries were very labour-intensive and child labour was plentiful and cheap, many writers tell us that without this availability the industrial revolution in Britain would not have been so successful. In the 1830s, when political reformers were trying to reduce the working hours of children in factories to ten a day, various objections were put forward. One of these was that the shorter hours would bring reduced wages and more family hardship. Another objector said that the profits on the job were only made in the last half hour of the day's work. If the length of the working day was reduced many firms would be ruined. It would also mean a loss of trade, which would pass to foreign competitors. To this last suggestion a supporter of the Bill said: 'A most surprising discovery has been made, namely, that our superiority over other nations is owing to 30,000 little girls in Lancashire . . . if these little girls work two hours less in a day than they do now, it would occasion the ruin of the country.'

A report of 1841 contains an interview with a 64-year-old skilled nail-maker, Thomas Billingham of Cradley Heath, which contains some very important information. He firstly mentioned that in Cradley Heath women, girls and boys made light chain, called 'swimmers' because these chains went over the water to other nations, particularly to America. (This description of the chain that was being made at the number of chain-shops located at Reddal Hill, between Old Hill and Cradley Heath, was used by officials of the Northern Chain Unions when they paid a fact-finding visit in 1858.) He then remarked that, since machines had been introduced to do weaving and spinning, the proportion of girls working in the nail and chain trade had increased tenfold, 'ten now, to one then', he said. He also commented that this was bad for the trade and bad for the girls. He said that when he was a boy (he was born in 1777) 'he rarely saw a girl making nails or chains, there are as many girls as boys now'. He added that children mostly worked with their own families and that those who did not were 'hired out' at so much a day or a week. Starting at 2–3*s* a week at first, they blew the bellows and 'dollied' the chain, the money being passed on to their parents.

He had himself hired out his three sons for a period of three years for the making of chain. The eldest son had worked with him at home making nails until he was sixteen years old. He then 'had the lawyer fellows of Dudley make out the articles'. The eldest son was hired out for 7*s* per week for the first year, 8*s* for the second and 10*s* for the third year. The second son being

A good illustration of the presence of children in working chain-shops. Before the youngsters were of school age the women had no alternative but to take their kids to work with them if there was no one to look after them at home. The woman in the right-hand corner is working so fast that she appears as a blur on the photograph.

only fourteen years old when he 'put him out', was hired for 6*s* for the first year, 7*s* for the second and 8*s* for the last. He said that none of the boys who were hired out actually lived with the masters: they were all 'out prentices'. Girls were never apprenticed out, but were only hired by the week. He noted that the masters did not beat the boys much at that time because their parents were near at hand, and would not stand it. He also commented that when he was a boy there were no Sunday schools for learning to read and write and he was nine years old before the first school was opened in the parish.

In the same report is mention of the youngest chain-maker that I have seen recorded. The inspector met him while passing through Cradley Wood (this would probably be Saltwells Woods) as he was on his way to see Thomas Holloway at the Salt Wells. As they walked along the lad, Thomas Barnsley aged 8½ years, talked freely to him. The boy explained that he had worked at chain-making since he was four years old. He said that 'I dolly and blow'; this

The small child up in the corner looks almost doll-like. This is a back-of-the-house chain-shop and the chain-maker is probably the little girl's grandmother. The bellows to supply blast to the hearth is quite visible on the left-hand side.

meant that he blew the bellows to keep the fire in the hearth going and then he would hammer on the 'dolly', the pivoted tool which was used to finish off the chain-link. He said that he got up at three, four and five in the morning, but never after three on a Saturday. He did not go to work until noon on a Monday. His pay was 3*s* 6*d* a week and sometimes 4*s* a week. He said that he always got his wages every week whether he worked regularly or not and the reason for this was because he worked for his uncle.

Several boys were interviewed who worked at the Henry Wood works. One described it as 'Mr Wood's Manufactory' and another as 'Masters Wood Brothers Works'. The one who gave his age as 'going on 13' said that 'he went to work at 6 in the morning and finished at 5, or half past 6 in the evening'. For this he was paid 3*s* a week, which he gave to his mother. Another boy said that he was 'going on 10' and that he 'worked at striking with his uncle and that some of the men had 4 or 5 boys under them, that is those who made big chains'.

Outworkers

Various terms were used to describe chain-makers who did not manufacture chains inside a factory, employed by and under the direct control and supervision of a chain-master or chain-works owner or, as they were usually known in the Black Country, 'a gaffer'. Under the Factory & Workshop Act of 1901, chain-masters or factors were required to fill in a 'Form 44'. I have in my possession a copy of one of the forms dated May 1907 made out by Jones & Lloyd of Cradley. This form, when completed, listed all the people, men, women and, I presume, children as well, who made chain in their own or a neighbour's workshop, or brewhouse chain-shop. The iron rods that they needed were either collected from or delivered by the chain-master or factor. The finished chains were then taken back to or collected by him and the chain-makers were paid for their work.

It is stated on Form 44 that it was the responsibility of the 'factory, workshop or place from where the work was given out to complete the form. A copy of the list, signed and dated and corrected up to that date, was to be forwarded to the local authority of the district on or before the first day of February and the first day of August in each year.' It was also stated that the list should be 'open to inspection by HM Inspectors and the officers of the local authority'. Form 44 contains columns in which are listed the outworker's name, brief address, and in another column a lower-case letter. The letters identified the trades followed by the outworkers. Those related to the Black Country industries in question were making of iron and steel cables and chain; making of iron and steel anchors and grapnels; and making of cart gear, including swivels, rings, loops, gear buckles, mullin bits, hooks and attachments of all kinds.

A report in *The Chain Makers' Journal and Trades Circular* published in 1859 refers to a dispute involving the cutting of the bellows used by the chain-makers to blow their fires in the hearths. This action affected the chain-makers at the Henry Wood chain-works at the Lye. This was an early established works on the Stourbridge Road, listed as being started as early as 1780, though whether or not the business was engaged in the making of chain at this early date is not known. The company had several works in the area, one of which was established near to the present Cradley Heath railway station in about 1847. It is believed that the name of Woods Lane came about because of the company's presence in that area. This was sixteen years before the railway reached Cradley Heath. Wood later concentrated production at the large works at Saltney, near Chester, which was built in about 1847. Here, the company became world famous for its chain, cable-chain and anchors.

This report distinguishes between the different types of chain-makers by referring to them as 'in-door [or factory] hands and out-door hands'.

Sometimes the outworkers had to collect the iron rods from the chain-masters or chain factors, take them back to their chain-shops or brewhouse workshops, make up the chain to order and then take the finished products back to the chain-master's warehouse. Illustrations are to be found in magazines and gazettes, especially from the last quarter of the nineteenth century, of women chain-makers in the Cradley and Cradley Heath area carrying the finished chain back to the warehouse draped around their neck and shoulders with heads bowed under the weight of the unwieldy load. This practice was confirmed by a couple who came to see chain being made by hand at the preserved Mushroom Green chain-shop in October 1993. The lady, who was in her late seventies, told me that one of her duties for her mother was to 'fetch the iron and take the chain back draped around my shoulders; that is why I walk with a stick now'. She said that she originally came from Cradley.

Some outworkers had the 'luxury' of a dobbin or hand-cart. This was sometimes known as a 'Fogger's Dobbin' or nicknamed a coffin on wheels, which was an apt description. It consisted of a wooden box about 18in wide at the top, tapering down to 15in at the bottom and 39in long at the top mounted on to a frame with a 4ft long handle which was fitted with a pair of spoked cartwheels, 30in in diameter. The overall length of the hand-cart was around 7ft 4in, and the width around 2ft 8in. This measurement of width was to allow the cart to pass easily up a 3ft wide house entry, a common feature of the rows of houses in the chain-making areas that had been built with chain-shops at the rear. The long handle was necessary to accommodate the iron rods that were carried which were between 8ft and 12ft long. These bars were usually cut in half before commencing to make the lengths of chain when 'working from the bar' as many of the outworkers did. The rods, when carried, rested on top of the dobbin box. A preserved example, which was saved by Ewart Chapman and can be seen in the Mushroom Green chain-shop, has a series of grooves in the top edges of the box which have been worn in by the regular carriage of many rods of iron over the years. When the order was completed the finished chain was carried back to the chain-master in the box part of the cart.

A 'bundle' was a recognised unit of weight that was accepted by both the iron suppliers and the chain outworkers. It weighed 56lb (some references

Here, in 1973, while working in his father's forge just outside Old Hill, Michael Bradney completed an order for ornamental chain to be installed around the rose gardens in front of Cardiff Castle. The cast-iron ornamental pointed parts were supplied and Michael had the job of connecting them together using wrought iron.

Chain-maker Michael Bradney can be seen here joining one half of a steering chain to the centre piece for use on an Aveling steamroller by means of a fire-welded link. His father, Arthur, who comes from a long line of Black Country chain-makers, can be seen sitting in the background in the preserved Mushroom Green chain-shop. The object pointing at Michael's head on the left is the top tool of the tommy-hammer. *(Ron Moss)*

mention 60lb), two bundles making a hundredweight. The bundle could also be divided into 8 quarters of 7lb each. To allow for scale and any wastage of iron during manufacture, the outworker was expected to return 52lb of chain to the chain-master, middleman or factor. Obviously the more thrifty chain-maker, and this included most of them, would join or fire-weld the remaining waste pieces together and make a few more links that would earn a few more coppers. I have also been told that the wire that held the bundles together was sometimes made into very small chain for use as dog-chain, etc.

In his book *The Sweated Trades* (1978) Duncan Bythell gives an illustration of outworkers in nineteenth-century Britain, citing as an example the firm of Eliza Tinsley of Old Hill (still trading). He states that in 1876 the entire production of this firm was carried out by between 1,800 and 2,000 outworkers, consisting of 600 adult men, 400 adult women and 800 young persons under the age of 18. Both the nail- and chain-makers were supplied weekly with bundles of iron from various warehouses situated around the area. By the end of the 1880s this total had fallen to between 1,200 and 1,500 outworkers with only about half of this number carrying out work exclusively for Eliza Tinsley; the remainder carried out work for other firms in the district at the same time.

One reason for this was that by this time 15 per cent of Tinsley's production was coming from their own workshop. This situation gradually changed as more and more work was carried out 'on their own ground' with less work being 'put out'. Even so I believe outworkers were still producing for Eliza Tinsley into the early 1950s.

John Burnett (Labour Correspondent of the Board of Trade), reporting on the chain district in November 1888, said that the 'factory system' had been introduced 'a little more than 50 years ago'. He also mentioned that a David Jones FGS had reckoned that in 1866 the number of persons employed in the chain trade in both factories and domestic workshops was about equal, with 2,000 men and boys employed in factories and 2,000 women and children working in 300 domestic workshops in the district; 50,000 tons of chains and cables were being produced annually plus another 10,000 tons of chain traces and country work.

By the time of Burnett's report in 1888 the number of workers making small-chain had more than doubled. Many outworkers had changed their trade from nail-making, which had been on the decline since machine-made nails started to appear in the 1830s. These workers would have been able quickly to adapt their domestic workshops and their skills of working iron in the fire to the making of small-chain.

An attempt to improve the lot of the chain-makers in domestic shops was reported in the *Birmingham Post* of 18 February 1889. An Arthur H.D. Acland of the Central Co-operative Board appealed for help through the newspaper in starting a Co-operative Chain-makers' Association at Cradley Heath. He said that it must be difficult and unprofitable to carry on the system of 'out-shops' (this is the earliest reference which I have seen to this description of a domestic workshop). He referred to Burnett's 1888 Board of Trade Report which had brought to the notice of the public the conditions under which the small-chain outworkers were trying to earn a reasonable living wage and said that one suggestion was to replace the domestic workshops with a co-operative factory system.

A later article dated 31 August 1889 in *The Co-operative News*, brought to my attention by Ned Williams, gave more details of the setting-up of a Co-operative Chain Factory in Cradley Heath. The idea was to raise the sum of at least £1,000 (a small fortune in those days when an outworker would be lucky to earn a few shillings in a week) by means of shares of £1 each 'to enable an experiment of this nature to be tried'. It went on to say that the Committee of the Central Co-operative Board, after further consideration, thought that a figure nearer to £2,000 would be needed to make a successful beginning. It was made clear that the money would not be required until a proper opening presented itself and for the moment people were asked to apply for shares. There then followed a surprisingly long list of interested bodies. These ranged from lords, dukes and earls to various individuals and also a long list of Co-operative Societies throughout the land from Newcastle-upon-Tyne to Cambridge. At the time of the article a total of £849 had been pledged.

The article contained a testimonial from a 'manufacturer of great experience' which 'is of the highest value' saying that it would be a good idea to establish a factory to make small-chain to supersede the present system of domestic workshops, which was a 'wasteful and evil system'. This manufacturer went on to say that the system had 'grown up in a large degree through the laxity of the Workshop Act, and the stringent enforcement of the Factory Act'. He ended by remarking that the chain trade was in a healthy state but suffered from the adverse conditions under which it was conducted.

The idea seems to have faded away quietly as no other record has been found of its development and the domestic workshops certainly continued to make the small types of chain by hand and did not begin to decline until the late 1920s and early 1930s, when more and more small-chain was made in larger workshops containing half a dozen or more hearths. Many lasted until after the Second World War. Certainly with the introduction of electrically welded steel chain by Samuel Woodhouse & Sons of Corngreaves Road, Cradley Heath, in 1903, small electrically welded chain had to be manufactured in a factory because of the capital cost of the machinery required to make it.

Chapter 3

Chain Shops, Tools, Techniques and Testing

The majority of Black Country chain-shops were built of common bricks, the colour range of which varied from medium red to purple and blue. I have heard them referred to as 'Black Country brindle' yet the dictionary tell us that this is a 'brownish-grey' colour. The bonding of the brick courses varied from shop to shop. Mushroom Green for instance has three courses of stretchers to one course of headers on the end walls while the side walls are constructed with anything from three to seven courses of stretchers to one course of headers. The majority of roofs were covered with 'Dreadnought' clay tiles manufactured at the Hinton, Perry & Davenhill works at nearby Pensnett. Most of them proudly displayed the name Dreadnought which was impressed on the underside face while in the unfired, soft state. The colour range of these tiles varied from medium to dark red. The tiled roofs projected a few inches over the outside walls of the chain-shops and very rarely have I seen them fitted with guttering to drain away the rainwater. This task was left to the small projection of the tiles which caused the rainwater to fall clear of the side walls. The roofs were generally hipped and finished off with clay ridge tiles along the apex. Many shops that were sited on their own or were to be seen included in a works complex were built on the 'lean-to' pattern, the higher part of the roof being against the boundary wall.

I have a copy of some handwritten questions and answers on the design of chain-shops which have been dated to around 1889. Various names appear above the list of questions, the first one being that of a Mr Juggins who was the secretary of the Midland Counties Trade Federation. The size and condition of chain-shops is dealt with in question 10. The question is posed as follows: 'Ten people work in a shop [chain-shop], is there plenty of room?' The answer is: 'No, very low workshops, ill ventilated and very insanitary.' The

General scene inside the Noah Bloomer chain-shop on a Saturday morning when most of the chain-makers had gone home.

recommendation is that the shops 'Must be 50ft long and 15 to 17ft wide; all open [opening] windows, See back.' On the reverse was written: 'Shops, height to wall plate or eaves 8 to 9ft. Width, 14 to 16ft. Men's fires 11ft apart and women's 9ft 6in apart.'

To see how these figures related to an actual example, just before the demolition of a property in Old Hill in May 1972 I was able to survey and record a pair of chain-shops at the rear of 5 and 6 Elbow Street. This was an area that had many chain- and nail-shops. Later, when looking at the dimensions of the hearths, I noted that the working height (from the floor to the hearth plate where the tongs are usually rested, level with the fire) varied from shop to shop by as much as 6in. Although these shops were side by side and appeared at first glance to be one structure they were separated by a brick partition wall and each had its own two-part 'stable-door'. I came to the conclusion that the first shop with the higher hearth working level was a men's chain-shop while the second was a women's chain-shop. All equipment had long since been removed from the shops leaving behind just the brick hearths. The presence of the remains of some tommy-stumps or ash poles in the shop would have confirmed the fact that one of them was a men's chain-shop.

Another question posed on the same sheet was from the Revd H. Rylett, the vicar from Dudley who took quite an interest in domestic nail- and chain-shops in his parish in the late 1880s. His question, number 25 on the sheet, was: 'Women and girls should not be engaged upon those sizes [of chain] that require the use of the foot.' This was a reference to the treadle-operated tommy-hammer which was used by the men when making sizes from ⅜in diameter upwards. The answer given was 'No such cases known'. In fact women were generally restricted to making up to ¼in diameter although some did make larger chain. These women are referred to in one book as 'Amazons'.

One feature that helps to identify the difference between a typical nail-shop and a domestic or small chain-shop is the position of the hearths in the shop. A nail-shop has its hearth set in the centre of the shop allowing several members of the family (or other workers) to work around it. If it contains more than one hearth they are usually arranged down the centre of the shop. A chain-shop has its hearths placed around the outer walls with one chain-maker occupying a hearth or in the case of 'dolly' chain-making (known locally as 'uphond, for two men') a chain-smith would have a striker (wielding a large sledgehammer) working with him.

The roofs were generally supported by queen- or king-post roof trusses. Some smaller shops and ranges of hearths in some of the works were covered by roofs of the lean-to variety, the lower part of the roof sloping down to the front yard. The typical chain-shop entrance was of the stable-door type, having the top and bottom halves opening independently so that light and air could be admitted through the top half while the bottom half, when closed, would keep out draughts, stray animals and children.

Window openings in the brickwork usually contained a stout wooden frame fitted with vertical round iron bars ½–¾in in diameter, set at about 4½in centres in the frame. The outside of the frame was furnished with a pair of strong wooden shutters fitted with straight bands pivoted on to the frame by a driven-in (hinge) hook. It was the common practice to fit the top hook upside down so that the shutter could not be easily lifted off. The shutters were normally closed when work was finished for the day but during the day they could be opened according to the prevailing wind and temperature. The windows were not glazed. Some brewhouse chain-shops had their shutters on the inside of the shop and operated in wooden slides. Window openings were dictated by the position of the adjoining buildings. Many simple lean-to chain-shops had a plain wall at the back without any window openings.

The Denholms: A Remarkable Iron-Forging Family

There were several families who devoted all their lives to the Black Country chain industry; one of these was the Denholm family. From an early notebook that I had the pleasure to look through, and conversations with the third generation of the family in the 1990s, I learnt that one Walter Ambrose Denholm left Poplar in London on a train at 5.30 a.m. on 14 October 1893 and arrived at Brierley Hill station at 12.30 p.m. He had been employed at one of the large London chain firms, possible Brown-Lenox or the Thames Ironworks, and as was typical in those days he started work in the chain-making department of the Earl of Dudley's Round Oak Works on the following Monday, 16 October 1893. I have not been

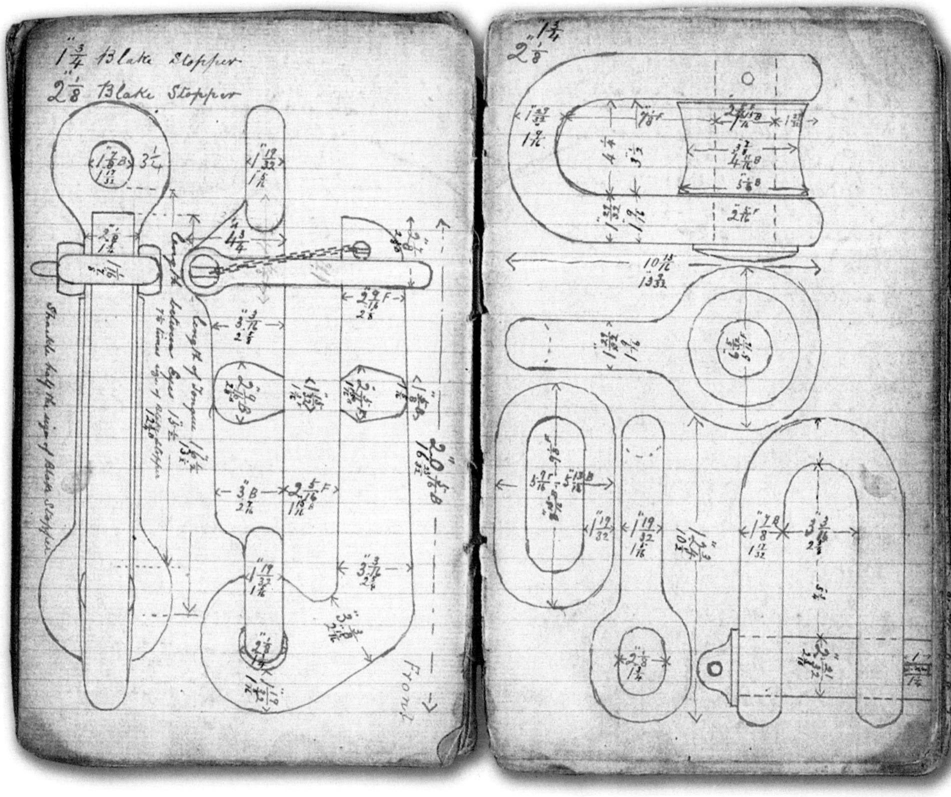

(Pages 64 and 65) Pages from the notebook of a succession of Denholm forgemen, who made chain and anchors in the Black Country from 1893 up to 1960. The object to be made would first be drawn out and the various sizes of metal that were required would be calculated. Usually the customer would also require a quote of the possible cost of the object to be made; this would also be worked out by the forgeman.

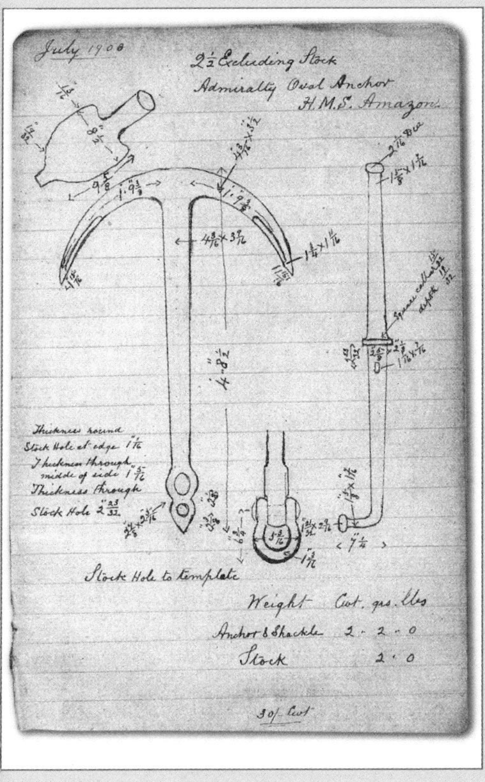

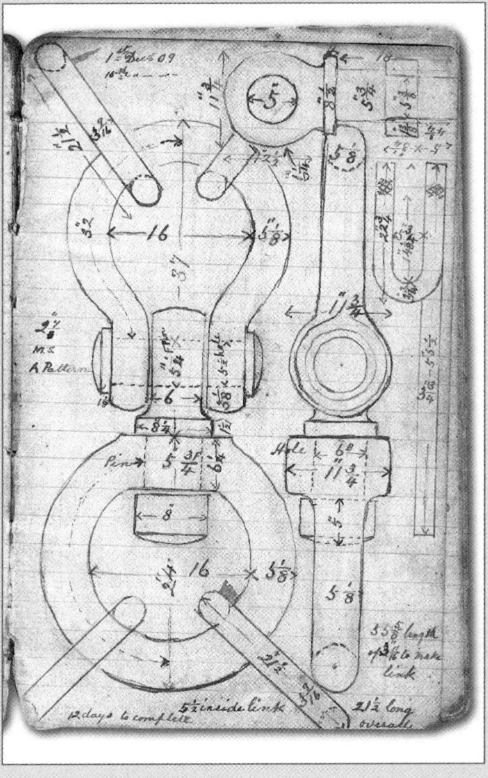

able to establish exactly when, but he later moved to the Noah Hingley Ironworks. He became chief smith and made large chain and anchor attachments until he died, before retirement, in 1917.

Following in his father's footsteps, his son, Walter Douglas, took over his position. Owing to his exceptional war effort working on chains and anchors during the Second World War, he was awarded the British Empire Medal and retired in 1953. Once again son followed father and Walter's position was taken over by his son, Robert. He worked on anchor adaptors and attachments, shackles and other fittings until Noah Hingley discontinued making large chain in the summer of 1960. Several members of the Denholm family also worked in this department, which was referred to as 'the Denholm shop'.

I had many chats with Bob and learnt a lot about the special items that are needed to equip a ship with anchor and mooring chains. I was able to study and copy many pages of the Denholm notebook that was started by Walter Ambrose around the beginning of the twentieth century. It was made good use of by his descendants, and of course they added to it, and it can be seen from the drawings and dimensions that as ships became larger and larger so did the fittings that were needed to equip them. One of the great values in the book *(continued on p. 66)* was the note made of the length of metal required to make a particular shackle or the parts for a mooring swivel. These calculations would originally have been arrived at by experiment and experience and the note of dimensions made then would serve the following family members in later years.

Also in the book are recorded lists of prices per hundredweight of the shackles, anchors and swivels, which are based on the time taken to make them. This information would be required by the office for sending an estimate to, or invoicing, the customer. Several smiths from the large firms to whom I spoke told me that, when an order was received by the firm, the 'gaffer' or one of the staff would come down to the department, or the smith would be invited to pop up to the office to advise on the cost of producing the various special items, or even the larger sizes of chain, so that the right price could then be passed on to the customer.

Some of the complex pieces of equipment mentioned in the Denholm notebook besides anchors, with their stocks and shackles, are senhouse slips, mooring swivels 'on Sir Thomas Hardy's plan', buoy shackles, deck stopper shackle and thimble and Blake, claw and clear house stoppers.

The number of famous ships' names mentioned, besides the *Titanic* and *Olympic*, is virtually never ending, including such as *Mauretania*, *Lusitania* and *Empress of Britain*, and Royal Navy ships such as the *Amazon* and others.

The floors of chain-shops were either a loose mixture of earth, cinder and ashes or consisted of common house bricks laid loosely on their widest side, any gaps between them rapidly being filled with the ash and cinder which were deposited from the hearth fires. Quite often, as was the case of the Mushroom Green chain-shop, the floor appeared to consist of black cinder and ashes but underneath this layer, when checked, was found a loose-laid brick floor. After a few years of use these brick floors, which were simply laid directly on to the earth below, became very uneven. One old nail-shop complex that I visited in the late 1960s appeared, at first sight, to have been constructed with its floor level 12–18in below the yard ground level outside. I was told by the gentleman working inside the shop that it had been operated by his family for over a hundred years. The nail-makers had simply thrown the unwanted ash and cinder out of the windows and doors on to the yard outside, so raising the level of the yard by more than a foot. I have seen several chain-shops since with the same feature. The working position near the hearth in a nail-shop was sometimes referred to as a 'pew', while that in a chain-shop was called a 'stand'. Mentions can be found sometimes where a worker states that he or she has rented a stall or pew in a workshop, paying the owner several shillings every week.

When a former chain-shop is located it is possible, if one looks up at the roof, to determine the number of hearths it contained and therefore how many workers earned their living there by counting the chimneys. Most chain-shops built before 1890 appear to differ from later examples in the construction of their chimneys. Starting from inside the shop, just above the stepped back brickwork above the fire and continuing out through the roof the bricks were laid 'on edge', that is on the 3in dimension of the brick, so forming a brick course 4½in deep. The sides of the chimney were built up using one brick on edge on two opposite sides and two bricks on edge on the other side; this means that alternate courses overhang around 1½in each side because they will not bond together. This gives a very distinctive and attractive appearance to the chimneys, a sort of crenellated vertical edge.

I have endeavoured over the years to find out the reason for this type of construction. One explanation given to me was that it produced a smaller internal size to the chimney thereby creating a better draught or draw to the fire. This is not really necessary because the breeze (small coke) fire in a chain-shop had air forced to it by a blower or bellows. A second explanation was that the Blackcountryman, never one to waste money unnecessarily, found that using bricks on edge meant that three courses of bricks raised his chimney by about 14½in whereas using them conventionally raised the height of his chimney by only 10in. A third suggestion is a good explanation. I was told that when lime mortar was used in the early days of building construction, the fairly constant heat passing up the chimney and the ravages of the weather in its exposed position caused the mortar in the chimney to dry up and return to dust. Chimneys built in the conventional manner would then collapse, damaging roofs and injuring workers inside or passers-by. When built with the brick on edge with the overhanging corners it resembled the construction of a log cabin and, if the mortar did dry out and fail, the chimney would still remain in place.

This would also account for the fact that chimneys built on chain-shops after about 1890 were built in the conventional manner using the bricks with a 3in course. This produced a square-cornered chimney and it also coincided with the increased use and availability of cement mortar, because as the cement became cheaper and was used more often a stronger and more weatherproof joint was formed.

A noticeable feature of many chain-shops and chain-works was the cast-iron pulley wheel, around 12in in diameter, located in a heavy wooden frame in which it could revolve on a spindle, the whole lot set in the brickwork, either

The end gable of the Quarry Bank Works of Noah Bloomer proudly telling the world that it was established way back in 1850.

over the door of the chain-shop or in an outside wall. This was simply to facilitate the loading of lengths of small-chain up to, say, ⅜in in diameter on to a lorry or wagon that would be drawn up beneath it. By attaching a small length of rope on to the end of the chain to be loaded and passing it over the pulley from the inside of the shop into the hands of a man standing on the back of a wagon or lorry, the length of chain would then be effortlessly loaded. Quite often the chain went right into a wooden barrel, especially if it was to be exported, as a lot of Black Country chain was. The advantage of this method would be best appreciated when the wheel was positioned in the solid outside wall of a chain-shop, or a test or inspection shop set around a yard (as can be seen at the original works of John Griffiths in Mushroom Green). It dispensed with the trouble of a horse-drawn wagon being manoeuvred through a restricted opening into a yard that might be obstructed by loads of fuel, iron rods or other materials.

When large side-welded chain was being made the chain-makers worked under a roof supported by wooden or iron pillars. The sides were left completely open to allow a cooling cross flow of air through the shop because of the terrific heat involved in the heating and welding of large pieces of metal.

I have been told that in the depths of winter corrugated sheets of metal were erected along the sides to keep out the icy winds. Some shops that were used to work and weld large pieces of hot metal can be recognised by the sets of wooden slatted louvres running across the roof for ventilation.

Fuel for the Hearth: Breeze

The type of fuel generally used by chain-makers was breeze, sometimes referred to as coke-breeze. Elihu Burritt, in his highly descriptive book *Walks in the Black Country* (1868), mentions this fuel and describes it as the fuel used by nail-makers. He said that they used a kind of coke they called 'breezes', but which doubtless should be spelt brises (the French word for breeze is *brise*, pronounced 'breez'), or 'broken bits of coal that have already passed through the fire'. They paid 6–7*d* per sack for these breezes, each sack containing around three bushels.

Coke is produced by burning coal in a closed chamber while excluding air from the chamber. The volatile ingredients of the coal are driven off leaving carbon combined with various gases and a small proportion of incombustible ash. In the production of 'coal gas' at the local gas works, before the coming of North Sea natural gas, one of the by-products after the gas and tar had been removed was large quantities of coke. Where 'pure' fuel was required, when smoke was to be avoided, then coke was the favourite and most suitable fuel. The gas-works in the chain-making areas of the Black Country certainly had plenty of customers for the coke.

It was a small size of coke, which today would be described as 'smokeless fuel'. In his excellent book *The Iron & Steel Industry, A Dictionary of Terms* (1971), Keith Gale tells us that it is 'screened (riddled) out of blast-furnace coke'. The coke used in blast furnaces must, out of necessity, consist of decent-sized lumps, but it was also produced by deliberate crushing. To enable the chain-maker to get a good clean fire-welded joint in his chain-link, the breeze was usually washed to remove dust or dirt. If dirt or scale was present when the two ends of the link were hammered together then the join would obviously not be clean and could prove faulty under test and possibly break.

The size of breeze used by the chain-makers depended on the size of chain which was being made. If the chain rod being used was between ¼in and 5/16in in diameter, then the most suitable size of breeze to use on the hearth would be pieces roughly in this same size range. Chain-makers producing ½in diameter chain would use breeze of roughly the same size while those making ¾–⅞in diameter chain would prefer breeze of equal size. The largest size of breeze, about 1in, was used by 'side-welders' who made the large cable-chain.

Sometimes the 'gleeds' or pieces of partly burnt coal from fires were used, especially by the small-chain makers, most of whom were women. Some gleeds were obtained by throwing shovelfuls of ash on water, often a convenient nearby pool or canal. The usable gleeds would float on the surface of the water and could be skimmed off while the remainder would sink to the bottom. This method, when used on the canals, sometimes meant that after a while the canal became silted up causing loaded boats to ground on the bottom, and so this practice had to be discouraged by the authorities concerned.

At the large works of Noah Hingley at Netherton lots of waste ash and cinders were by-products of the many fires and furnaces on their site. The value of these was realised and the waste from the fires was wheel-barrowed across a bridge over the nearby canal and tipped into an iron tank 'the size of a living-room', Bob Denholm of Noah Hingley told me, and here two women were permanently employed in skimming off the floating breeze in the tank, which was then carried back into the works and used by the chain-makers as fuel in their hearths.

Small chain-makers, working in backyard brewhouse chain-shops, sometimes purchased their breeze from a local supplier. I have been told that one such dealer in Old Hill sold it by 'the bucket-full'. A white enamel bucket was used as a measure and I was told by one man, who as a child was sent to collect breeze for his parents and grandparents, that a round block of wood, 2–3in thick, was fixed into the bottom of the bucket and painted white. This meant that the poor chain-maker was cheated out of a few pennyworth of fuel with every delivery. The cost of a bucket-full, when my informant collected it in the early 1930s, was 4*d.*

While on the subject of fuel, it is worth mentioning that chain-makers in other parts of the country have used certain types of coal. At Brown-Lenox and Co. at Pontypridd, South Wales, small coal or 'slack' was used. This was also adopted at the works of Noah Hingley at Netherton on certain jobs. The fires were given the name of 'slack-fires'. When large links or shackles or anchor parts were being made, special fires were made up in hearths using solid tuyers (that is not hollow and water cooled) and 'Bargoed slack' from South Wales as the fuel. Bargoed slack had qualities that meant it coked freely. Walls of fuel were built up and, while the breeze or coke from the previous day was being burnt to provide the great heat needed on large objects, the Bargoed slack behind it was being turned into coke by the nearby heat so that it could be used as the fuel during the next day.

It must be noted that coke and breeze fires need a good blast of air to keep them going. Once the blast is turned off, the fire will die down and appear to

This chain-shop on the side of Butchers Lane, Cradley, was threatened with housing development and demolition in July 1975 and the Industrial Archaeology Group of the Black Country Society worked hard with Albert Nock, its owner, to save it. Chain had last been made here in 1941. In July 2001 it was again threatened with demolition and housing development. Mr Nock had passed away in 1992 and the shop came into the ownership of his niece, Mrs Hazel Tromans. Through the hard work of Mrs Norma Ridge, headmistress of Temple Meadow Primary School, and a very interested and dedicated party of helpers, and the generosity of Mrs Tromans, the chain-shop was moved in 2001 and reconstructed in the grounds of the school.

go out, but even if it is ignored for twenty minutes or so (on a small-chain maker's hearth), it needs only a few minutes of air-blast to get it going again.

The price of breeze is mentioned in R.H. Tawney's *Minimum Rates in the Chain Making Industry* (1914). His research was carried out in the one or two years before the publication of his book when he learned that some of the forge workers purchased their breeze from hawkers who went from chain-shop to chain-shop selling it in baskets; no weight is mentioned. In 1910, at the time of the Trade Boards enquiry, the breeze was sold at 3½*d* for one basket and 5½–6*d* for two baskets. It is believed that the dealers at that time were paying around 17*s* per ton for it. Between then and 1912 there had been a coal strike, one of the effects of which was the raising of the cost of breeze to between 30 and 40*s* per ton. By 1912, when the Trade Boards were again making enquiries, the price had fallen back to its previous level of around 17*s* per ton. However, the price being charged by the hawkers at that date was 7*d* for two baskets and 4½*d* for one.

Just a final note about breeze. With the run-down of the hand-made chain industry from the early 1960s the demand for breeze decreased. We then find that some of the same firms that supplied breeze as a fuel turned their hands to making another product, 'the breeze-block'. This was the first type of building block that was used for building internal walls in houses – as one early encyclopedia described it, 'in inexpensive buildings'. Ashes were mixed with cement and moulded into blocks.

Tools of the Trade

Like any specialised craft the chain-making business had its own particular tools and a unique vocabulary. Among the tools associated with chain-making were the oliver and the tommy hammer and the processes used included dollying and tommying.

The Oliver

The oliver is a simple, adaptable, versatile, very reliable manually operated treadle hammer. It allows the operator to strike blows upon the metal object being made while keeping both hands free either to guide or manipulate the metal being forged or deliver supplementary blows with a hand hammer at the same time. It is made up of various components, one of them being a cast-iron 'cube' having approximately 15in sides and containing various holes and slots for the location of blocks and tools that can be used in the manufacture of the variety of objects which can be made. When set up with the necessary tools, countless operations can be carried out including bending, shaping, drawing out, piercing and others. This iron cube usually rests on top of a block of stone, quite often a discarded natural grindstone, with a suitable piece of 'insulation' in between, such as a hessian bag or old leather apron. Two wooden stumps, the sizes of which vary in section according to the size of the hammers used or the weight of the objects that are to be forged, are buried deep in the floor. The parts of the oliver stumps below ground level are generally found to be the original tree trunks with the remaining 4 or 5ft above the ground having been sawn to the slightly oblong shape required. These stumps are fastened together with tie-bars and nuts that allow for the bearings between them to be adjusted. Metal strips are also used to secure the stumps to the work block. Between these stumps, pivoted by means of adjustable bearings, is an axle shaft upon which is fixed a large hammerhead of suitable weight. Quite often two axles are fitted, each having a hammerhead into whose square hole a variety of tools can be located that are suitable for carrying out a great many operations. If two

Here we have an excellent photograph of the working area in an odd-work shop. The most important piece of equipment here is in the centre of the picture. This is the oliver with its two ash spring poles above it. This treadle-operated hammer has been used in English forges since at least the fourteenth century. The hearth is on the left and the various interchangeable tools and dies are stored nearby. This photograph was taken at the Ewart Hackett Old Hill Works in May 1974 shortly before it closed. *(Keith Fellows)*

hammerheads are fitted, then two wooden treadles are required to operate them, and are connected to them by iron bars. One or two ash poles, or in later years one or two large (2½–3in diameter) metal springs, are employed to return the hammer heads to the upright position so as to be out of the way of the working area.

The oliver was still used until quite recently by the 'odd-work' maker, turning out quantities of various types of brackets, hooks, shackles and other items, in fact any object that it was not worthwhile setting up a large automatic machine for, the oliver could handle. It was also the favoured tool of the nail-maker who used it mostly for heading his nails, the finished nail being ejected from the 'bore' by a pivoted lever located in one of the slots in the front part of his working block that he struck with his hammer at the end of the operation.

From the oliver, the chain-maker developed the 'tommy hammer', which differed only slightly from the oliver in that a wooden box containing packed down ashes and cinders took the place of the iron block and stone. On top of these ashes and cinders was placed a 3–4in thick working block into which the chain-maker located his or her tools (see drawing p. 79). For the making of large 'tommied' chain up to and around 1in in diameter, a cut wood log was set in the box, with the ashes and cinders packed around it. This would then help to take the heavier blows needed when working on the larger diameter metal.

The intriguing question of how a treadle-operated hammer became known throughout the engineering world as an 'oliver' has been asked many times over. A very good suggestion came to my notice in recent years from two different people living many miles apart following my lectures on chain-making.

F.J. Westwood of Halesowen suggested that the saying 'A Roland for an Oliver' might be the reason for calling the hammer an 'oliver'. Reference books tell us that 'A Roland for an Oliver', was a phrase or idiom that was used for 'tit for tat', or 'to give as good as one gets' and 'blow for a blow'. Expanding this theory, G.T. Badley of Southampton University Industrial Archaeology Society wrote an article that was published in *Focus*, the journal of that society, in July 1980 entitled 'New Batteries for Old', which cleverly dealt with the names that are given to new pieces of technology as they are invented. The 'oliver' is mentioned and, with a little extra information, the story goes thus:

Roland, the legendary nephew of the Emperor Charlemagne, had a companion knight who fought gallantly beside him in battles with the Saracens and others; his name was Oliver, and he was one of Charlemagne's twelve paladins. These two knights became heroes and their fame spread throughout Europe. Roland's deeds were immortalised in the French *chanson de geste*, the

A general view of a typical hand chain-maker's hearth showing the tommy hammer, the wooden stumps of which are buried into the floor about the same depth as can be seen above it. The maker has his foot on the treadle of the tommy and the hammer is about to strike the chain-link. The location is Mushroom Green Chain-shop.

Song of Roland, which was very popular in the Middle Ages. Oliver, although not very intelligent, was large in stature and courage and as strong as a horse. A valuable companion in battle, he would give blow for blow until his opponents were defeated. Badley goes on to say in his article: 'Many skilled smiths, sweating from the weight of their hammers must have wished for such a companion, an indefatigable repeater of hard, controlled blows. But who would want this dull, exacting job to have to be so alert to demands and yet, personally so subordinate and uncreative? No one, except a machine: and the machine, like Roland's companion, was an OLIVER.'

In a rearguard battle against the Basques, at Roncesvalles, in August 778, Roland perished with all his force. The date of the first recorded reference to the Knights Rouland and Oliuer (*sic*) was 1330, which pre-dates the early reference, in 1352 (if proved correct), to the oliver as a hammer by twenty-odd years.

A good illustration of a working hearth for hand chain-making. The chain-maker can be seen closing the link down and the chain that he is producing can be seen snaking along the floor in the right corner. The water bosh can be seen behind him and the tommy hammer in front of him, with the treadle very prominent in the front of the picture. *(By kind permission of Geoff Webb)*

An early reference to a treadle-operated hammer, working on the same principle as an oliver although not referred to by that name, is to be found in Robert Plot's *The Natural History of Staffordshire* (1686).

Robert Plot travelled around England in the seventeenth century, recording what he considered to be useful information about interesting and unusual tools and processes that he saw on his travels. In his book he describes how he found in a smith's shop, 'a little south of Mole Copp' in Staffordshire, 'an engine that managed a large sledg [a sledgehammer] to so great advantage, that it frequently supplyed [*sic*] the defect of a man ordinarily had elsewhere for that purpose'. An accompanying drawing shows the treadle hammer that he saw and appears to have very little difference in its layout to the oliver that was still in use some 200 years later in forges and odd-work shops.

Almost 100 years later another traveller, also recording his observations, provides us with a drawing that is easily recognisable as an oliver. In 1770 Arthur Young noted the presence of a treadle hammer at Kiplin in the North Riding of Yorkshire. He recorded the fact in his book *A Six Months' Tour through the North of England.*

In 1702 Ralph Thoresby, the Yorkshire antiquary, mentioned in his recollections, *The Diary of Ralph Thoresby*, that he saw a similar machine near Leeds. Each of these gentlemen made the point that the treadle hammer allowed one smith to carry out the work of two. Thoresby summed up the views of the three observers when he recorded: 'At Lofthouse, we saw a smith working with two hammers, one of which, by a pretty contrivance, (the first I have seen in these parts) he moved with his foot, that he had the use of his left hand to hold the iron, while he struck with his right, and the engine supplied the place of a labourer to strike with the great hammer.'

We have to move on to the mid-nineteenth century before the device that we call a 'foot-operated treadle hammer' is actually referred to for the first time in print as an 'oliver'. C. Holtzapffel, in his *Turning and Mechanical Manipulation*, published in 1856, tells us that 'the machine was used . . . in making long, stout nails'.

The oliver was used for the heading of nails by the many thousands of men, women and children engaged in the nail-making trade in the Black Country. This trade, always domestic in character, was recorded in Staffordshire as early as the reign of King John (1199–1216). Its decline came about when cut nails were produced by machine from around 1811 and followed soon after by headed nails. By the 1830s vast quantities of machine-made nails were being produced and the poor hand nail-maker could not compete on speed of production or price. The trade gradually dwindled away but some nailers could still be found in the 1950s, producing the large-headed specialist decorative types such as 'prison door' nails, working as outworkers for such companies as Eliza Tinsley & Co. of Old Hill, one of the oldest established nail firms in the Black Country.

Another Old Hill firm carried on using an oliver well into the 1980s for producing small quantities of various sizes of shackle pins.

The Tommy Hammer

I have been asked by many visitors to the Mushroom Green chain-shop over the years this question: why is the pivoted-spring treadle-operated hammer that was fitted next to most hearths in Black Country chain-shops universally known as a 'tommy hammer'? Even the chain-shops are often referred to as 'tommy shops'. Benjamin Disraeli mentions the operation of 'tommy shops' a number of times in his novel *Sybil* (1845).

I have yet to find any positive evidence to confirm it but in my opinion the name has a direct connection with 'truck' or 'tommy' money that was issued by some employers instead of money of the realm for wages. Some or part of the workmen's wages was paid in tokens or notes that could only be redeemed in the gaffer's own works shop. The goods in the shop, which included food, clothes and utensils, were usually not of high quality. However, to get the value of the tommy or truck the workers were forced to buy from the master. Parliament tried on many occasions to outlaw this practice and after many years it was finally stamped out. Perhaps the chain-makers decided to name their treadle-operated hammers 'tommy hammers' because the machine was helping them to earn their 'tommy money'.

Before the establishment of the small-chain making industry that was mainly carried on in small family domestic shops from the early nineteenth century, the same trouble was experienced by the poor nail-makers, probably from the early fifteenth century onwards.

While carrying out my early research in the 1970s many people told me that in their parents' lifetime they could remember tommy shops situated in their local areas. One was in Ash Street (formerly Bank Street), Old Hill, standing in front of the Hacket Bros oliver shop and another one was near the canal locks in Dock Street, Wordsley.

Joining the Links

The most common place to join or weld a link of hand-made chain is on the crown or the end; it is then described as 'end-welded chain'. The Chain Makers' & Strikers' Association price list dated March 1948 covers 'Admiralty Close and Open Link Chains, Catting & Steering Chains, Block or Pitch Chains, all Endwelded'.

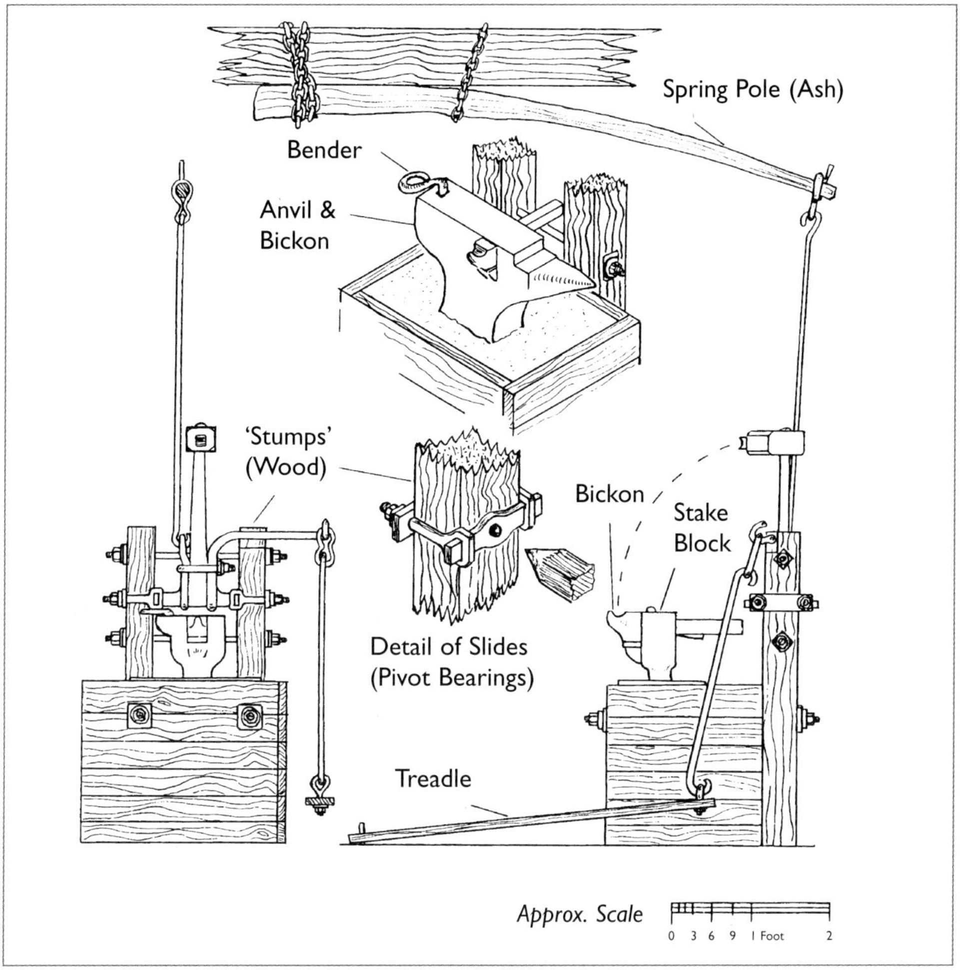

Typical chain-maker's tommy hammer. *(Ron Moss)*

All the small 'hammered' chain that was made by the women chain-makers was joined on the end and also all 'tommied' (the join finished and cleaned up on the tommy hammer) and 'dollied' (the weld finished using dolly tools). This is a very old process. During excavations at the site of the Roman town of Vindolanda close to Hadrian's Wall some very good examples of small 'indented chain' (the sides of the link being closed to help prevent knotting) that had been preserved in the boggy ground also showed signs of being welded on the end or crown of the link.

For convenience of working, the point at which the size of chain begins to be welded on the side of the link varies from factory to factory and also according to the year of manufacture. In Thomas Traill's marvellous book *Chain Cables and Chains* (1885) he states that 'When chains are side-welded, which they should be from about one inch upwards . . .' As the years pass by

Mushroom Green Chain-shop is one of the modern hands-on museum outposts and visitors are encouraged to have a go at making a chain-link. Here the author is seen doing just that in April 1977 shortly after the shop was opened to the public. The wood of the tommy stumps is still clean and the inside of the chain-shop has still to be whitewashed. *(Dave Whyley)*

the diameter at which side welding should commence appears to grow. A tape recording of two ex-Noah Hingley side-welders that I had the pleasure of listening to included their remarks that they tended to end-weld links up to $1^{13}/_{16}$in diameter and then from that size they would side-weld them. A lot of firms began the side welding of links at 2in diameter and upward. Traill, a naval officer, was incidentally the Inspector of Chain Cable and Anchor Proving Establishments and also General Superintendent, Lloyds Committee on Proving Establishments, as well as being the Engineer Surveyor-in-Chief at the Board of Trade.

A joint patent taken out by Samuel Brown of Mark Lane, London, and Philip Thomas of Liverpool, manufacturers of iron cables, described various attempts in 1816 to pre-form chain-links by winding the hot metal bar around a three-part mandrel (it then looked like a coiled spring) and then cutting the coils of metal diagonally across the side, after which they then welded them on the side.

The first chain-links to be side-welded in the Staffordshire and Worcestershire district are credited to Henry Pershouse Parkes of Tipton. He had been making chains since 1817 but it was 1825 before he manufactured his first cable-chain, his works then being sited in Dudley. He moved the few miles to Tipton and set up his new works to take advantage of the convenient canal system and it was here in 1840 that he turned out his first 1in diameter stud-link side-welded chain. At that time a cable-chain of 1⅝in diameter was considered to be very large. A little later, in 1849, Henry Wood & Co. of Saltney, Chester, commenced making stud-link cable-chain of 1¼in diameter, which he end-welded. Shortly afterwards he began manufacturing side-welded cable-chain of 1⅞in diameter and built up a world-wide

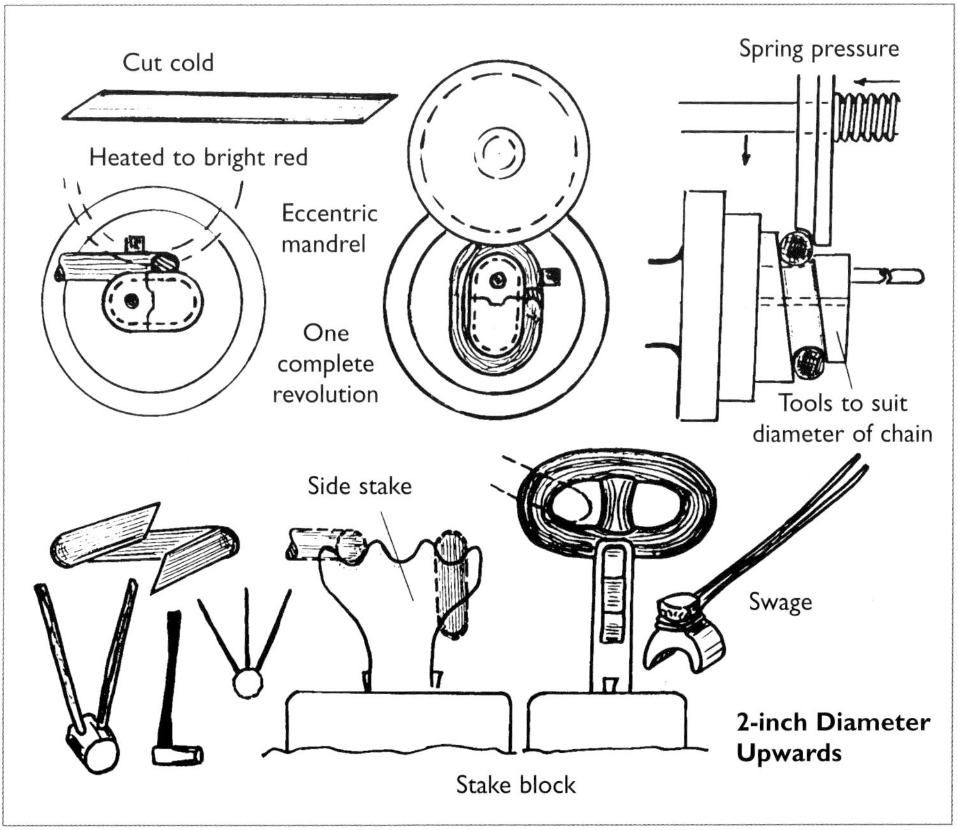

Tools used to make a side-welded chain. *(Ron Moss)*

reputation for making first-class chain. By 1912 Noah Hingley of Netherton was making sizes of cable-chain up to 5½in in diameter for use as anchor attachments for the ever-growing large luxury liners.

Dollied Chain

This method also involves the welding or joining of the chain-link on the end of the link and so technically it is also end-welded chain. This method is generally used for sizes over 1in in diameter to just below 2in in diameter.

It is always worth bearing in mind that different firms might vary the range in which this method of manufacture is used. I have found cases of some companies using a dolly for much smaller diameter chains than the range mentioned above.

One lady chain-maker told me that during the Second World War her firm had an order from the Admiralty for lengths of chain that were to be used for securing sea mines to the sea bed, which meant that these chains would spend all their life on the sea floor, and yet the Admiralty specified that the finished

A typical three-man dolly chain-making team recorded in March 1949, probably at Noah Hingley, Netherton. They are proudly showing their skills to some nattily suited visitors. The chain appears to be around 1¼in in diameter. *(Roy Baugh)*

welded join was to be 'dollied'. This meant smoothing out the hand-welded joins with a pair of hollow tools. I believe that this mine-anchoring chain was quite small, possibly around $^5/_{16}$ or $^3/_8$in in diameter.

A treadle hammer is not used with this method of manufacture but a bickon, very much like the type used on 'tommied' chain, having a radius equal to the diameter of the chain to be made forms the bottom tool while a hinged or pivoting top tool, again having a hollow tool on its end equal to the radius of the diameter of the chain to be made, is used for striking. The bottom tool passes through a square hole in the side of an anvil, the size of which can vary to suit the size of chain to be made. The anvil is usually chained and staked to a large log of wood, two-thirds of which is buried in the floor of the forge. This log gives a fair bit of resistance to the blows that are struck during the operations that are required to make the links of chain. It also cushions the force of the smith's hammer blows, so relieving his wrist and arm a little of pain. The top tool is fitted on to the back of this bickon by means of a 'dolly-box'. This has open bearings having no top bearing cover and is held down by weights, such as old chain-links. These are contained in a 'cage' made out of small diameter iron rod attached to the pivots. I found that the chain-makers' pet name for these odd links used as weights was 'jinglers' owing to the sound that they made as they danced up and down when a blow was delivered with the sledgehammer on the top tool. This sound is unmistakable to someone in the know when they walk into the yard of a chain-works. Many times I entered the Noah Bloomer yard in Quarry Bank on a Saturday morning and heard the sound of jinglers as I passed through the gate. I would dash over to the large hearth in the centre of the yard to try to capture on film this fast disappearing process of making chain using the dolly. The last time that I had the pleasure of watching dollied chain being made at Noah Bloomer of Quarry Bank was in January and February 1975, and this was on the last dolly hearth that was being used in the region.

When the processes of bending, scarfing and shutting the link have been carried out, the pivoted top tool, which contains a groove equal to the radius of the chain being made, is then gathered up and placed by the hand of the striker on top of the join of the link and then both the striker and chain-smith rain blows on the top tool, while the chain-smith turns the link about with his tongs until they are satisfied that the metal in the join is of the same diameter as the remainder of the chain-link and that all traces of the welded join are removed.

Sometimes a second groove, perhaps not so deep as the main one, is to be seen in the bottom tool. The link is located in this second groove when cable-chain is being manufactured and the groove ensures that no 'flat' appears on

Probably the last hearth in England, maybe even the world, to be making chain by the dolly method. Here, Clarrie Johnson (*left*) and Tony Jankowski are hard at work in 1975 at Noah Bloomer of Quarry Bank making lengths of chain that will be used as a chain sling. They are scarfing the ends of the U-shaped metal before closing the two ends together to make a chain-link.

the bottom of the finished link when hammer blows on the top using a hollow tool close it over the inserted stud. Many chain-makers have told me that the Admiralty would not accept chain that had flats on the links for the Royal Navy.

When making dollied chain the general rule was to use a chain-smith and a striker for sizes from around 1in in diameter up to $1\frac{5}{16}$in in diameter. For sizes from $1\frac{3}{8}$in up to just 2in in diameter a smith and two strikers were employed. Once again these ranges could vary from firm to firm. In the Black Country, making dollied chain with one striker was known as 'working uphond'; when two strikers were used it was known as 'working double'.

An interesting record contained in the Parliamentary Papers of 1843 described the process of making a chain-link using a dolly, but from the description it does not appear to be the same type of pivoted dolly that was used up to modern times. It described the tool like this: 'This is a kind of hammer, the head of which is a little arched, or concave, at the face or under part; and this being laid upon the iron, it is then struck upon the upper part of its head with hammers. By this means the rounded shape of the link is rapidly formed without many blows, or much turning of the links.' This sounds like a hollow tool or swage, the type of tool widely used in side-welding when finishing off the weld or setting down the side of the link upon the stud. This is held in the hand, and not in an open bearing, in a dolly-box which in turn is fitted on to a bickon as the dolly tool is. The description went on to say that 'A man with a heavy hammer in one hand, holding the link in a pair of tongs in the other hand, is assisted by a boy with a lighter hammer, who manages the dolly with his left hand.' The report explained that the man often worked with two boys but, when the chain was large, he sometimes had three or four boys or even as many as six. Some of the children were too small to be efficient and so blocks were placed around the anvil upon which 'the little creatures have to stand to deliver their blows'. The children were put to this work at the age of seven or eight, or as soon as they could use a hammer. One boy the inspector met, who 'looked more than usually strong for his years, had been put to chain-making at four years of age'.

Proving or Testing Chain

The importance of proving or testing cable-chain was realised by Samuel Brown (1776–1852), an officer of the Royal Navy. After retiring from active service he founded his own chain-making firm in 1803. In 1806 he formed a partnership with his cousin Samuel Lenox (Brown, Lenox & Co.) and he experimented widely in the manufacture of different types of iron cable-chains. To prove the superiority of iron cables over hemp ones, in 1809 he equipped a ship, the *Penelope*, with iron cables and carried out voyages to Martinique and Guadeloupe and back to prove their worth. In 1812 he set up a works at Millwall on the River Thames to manufacture ships' iron cable-chain. Sometime between 1812 and 1816 he developed a chain-testing machine. It was based on the principles that were to be used for testing chain for many years, principles that are broadly still in use today. The machine turned out to be very reliable and accurate and with its help Samuel Brown was able to discover any faults in the design and manufacture of chain or in the material that it was made from. He was able, therefore, to improve the quality of his products so much that his, and the country's, reputation for producing high-quality mooring chain grew throughout the world.

In 1847 ships still carried four iron cables but the hemp cables carried had been further reduced from three to two. The new rules of *Lloyds Register* for the year 1853 made it compulsory that, before a vessel could be classed, its owners were required to produce a certificate to prove that its cable-chain had been properly tested.

Meanwhile the Royal Navy issued a directive in 1854 to the effect that screw-propelled ships of the line had to be equipped with five iron cable-chains while hemp cables were reduced to just one. An alternative arrangement if this was not possible was to carry four iron cables and two hemp ones. This was a timely instruction because in the same year ships of the fleet found themselves in the Black Sea off Balaclava riding out a very severe gale; not one of them suffered a broken cable. Some merchant ships in the same area using hemp cables unfortunately suffered some loss of life among their crews.

In 1858 the committee of Lloyds laid down rules governing the length of cables and formulae standardising the size of chain-links. These formulae were based on the diameter of the iron from which the chain was made. With this move it is thought that the chain-making trade was the first trade to have its products standardised.

A select committee was appointed in 1860 to look into the manufacture of cable-chains and concluded that chains and anchors that had been properly tested and examined after manufacture rarely broke or parted so as to put their ships in danger. In addition they noted that, after a certain period of service, it would be wise to have chains and anchors re-tested. Up to this time most of the chains and anchors tested were for the use of the Royal Navy and it was thought that it would save a lot of lives and property if the testing was extended to equipment that was to be used in merchant vessels as well. When this was done it was found that cable-chains and anchors that were manufactured for merchant vessels were often made from inferior iron and were not subject to such stringent control of workmanship.

Hemp and Iron Cables

It is interesting to compare the sizes and weights of hemp and iron cables that were required to carry out the same task. One of the obvious ways is to match the breaking strains and working loads of both types of cable.

First of all let us look at the formulae for calculating these. These vary from book to book, but the one that I have found to be most reliable for rope is as follows: for the breaking strain, divide the square of its circumference in inches by 5, this gives the answer in tons, and to calculate the working or 'safe' load, divide this breaking strain by 6. If we take the example of 1in cable-chain, first remembering that the 1in measurement is the size of the iron bar that the chain-smith makes the chain from, the outside size of the links is 6in long by 3⅝in wide (BS3006:1949); this has a breaking strain of 27 tons and a weight of 54lb per fathom. The nearest equivalent hemp cable would be 11½in in circumference (just over 3⅝in diameter), having a breaking strain of 26.45 tons and weighing just over 30lb per fathom. One more example worth quoting is for 2in cable-chain, which must stand a breaking strain of nearly

A dramatic view of the large-chain test-bed at the Samuel Taylor Works, Brierley Hill. On test, when this photograph was taken, was a length of the special silicon-aluminium-bronze chain that is specially made for use on Royal Navy minesweepers.

101 tons. The equivalent hemp cable would have to be 22in in circumference or 7in diameter to reach a breaking strain of almost 100 tons (96.8 tons).

As ships were built larger and larger, the size of their anchor cables necessarily increased in order to cope with the extra tonnage involved.

Hemp cables became very cumbersome to handle, especially when they were 8in or 9in in diameter (some as large as 12in) and wet, which they usually were. They were difficult to stow, the room taken up by the later iron cable being roughly one-third of that taken up by hemp. This valuable space could be used for carrying revenue-earning cargo. The hemp cables were also prone to chafe under friction, or could be cut by coral in tropical waters, the same conditions merely polishing iron chain. They tended to rot from alternate wetting and drying out. During sea battles hemp was easily damaged by shot, shell and fire; iron was not so easily damaged. In winter, hemp cables were chafed and cut by ice. Iron cables had a much longer working life and also acted as ballast when vessels were travelling partly loaded or empty.

One of the reasons why the Navy was a little slow in adopting iron cables was because, if ships were surprised at their moorings and they had to 'cut and run' in a hurry, they could easily chop through their hemp anchor cable, sacrificing their anchor but allowing them to get away quickly. The invention of the quick-release shackle therefore helped to speed up the adoption of iron cable-chain by the Navy. Black Country legend has it that Sir Richard Sykes, a Cradley Heath chain-master, was knighted for the invention of the shackle. Shackles were usually employed to join together 12½-fathom lengths for the Royal Navy and 15-fathom lengths for the Merchant Navy. In later years the 15-fathom length seems to have been generally used.

Another use for iron cable-chain is mentioned in Douglas Lobley's book *Ships through the Ages* (1972). In the chapter dealing with the famous tea clippers of the mid-nineteenth century he relates the story of a race between three clipper ships in 1866 from Foochow in south-west China to London. He points out that clippers were very sensitive to the way that they were trimmed and as well as the cargo being loaded very carefully it was common practice to balance the ship by moving different lengths of cable-chain from the chain locker in the fo'c'sle to the stern.

Calculating Chain Strength

Laws and rules relating to the testing and use of chains have been in use since at least 1858 and various simple formulae have been devised to calculate the loads that the chains can be tested to and the safe loads that they can be used for. These formulae are based on one simple common measurement: no matter what size the chain might be, this is the diameter of the rod of wrought iron or steel that the chain-link is manufactured from.

As the quantity of puddled wrought iron being produced declined during the twentieth century, the type of metal used for making chain has been improved as regards its load-carrying capacity by the development of alloy steels of various types.

A large quantity of electrically welded small-chain was originally manufactured, and is still made, from a soft, low-carbon-content, mild steel that can be worked readily and welds well and serves its purpose. Apart from the excellent anti-corrosive and fire-welding qualities of wrought iron, partly due to the slag inclusions that are worked into it during its manufacture, this mild steel is a metal with very similar properties. In fact, referring to *The Chain Testers' Handbook* by C.H.A. McCaully (1973–4), we find that the 'yield stress' for wrought iron is 16 tons per square inch while that for 'dead soft mild steel', the material used for a large amount of steel chain, is 17 tons per square inch.

The same formula is actually employed for calculating the use loads for chain made out of these two similar materials. To find the tensile strain, or proof test load in tons, the formula $12d^2$ is used where d is the diameter in inches of the iron or steel used in the manufacture of the chain-links. The formula for finding the breaking strain or load which is usually applied to a sample three-link piece of short-link chain that may be taken from any part of the length of chain is $24d^2$. The safe working load or SWL can then be found by halving the tensile load, that is $6d^2$. The details for this can be found in BS394 and BS1696 for wrought iron and BS590 for mild steel.

Studded cable-chain has a slightly higher load test at $18d^2$ for the tensile test and $27d^2$ for the breaking test, the SWL being $9d^2$. Higher tensile steel has a tensile strain of $16d^2$, and a breaking strain of $40d^2$ and a SWL of $8d^2$. This is covered by BS1663. Alloy-steel chain, Grade 60, has a tensile strain of $24d^2$ and is covered by BS3113, while Grade 80 has a tensile strain of $32d^2$ and is dealt with in BS3114.

British Standard tables are available showing the tensile strain allocated to each size and grade of chain. These are graduated so that when the proof load is applied the chain just starts to stretch.

Test Certificates

In his book *Chain Cables and Chains* Thomas Traill reproduced examples of the test certificates that were issued by the various Lloyds proving houses. The first library copy that I saw of this book was a bound collection of photocopies of the original pages so when I saw an original example of the book some years later I was surprised and pleased to find that the test certificates were in different colours. Each proving house had certificates with the lettering printed in a colour allotted to that particular test establishment. Although the Netherton Proving House was not the first one to be established

British Chain-Makers in Germany

A very interesting story was related in the souvenir book of the Chain Makers' and Strikers' Association on the celebration of their twenty-fifth anniversary on 6 July 1914. The story carried the mysterious heading 'The Plot that Failed'. It told the story of an attempt by a German rolling mill and chain manufacturer, located on the banks of the Rhine at Duisburg, to learn the finer art of making chain by hand – commentators had previously noted that the art of cable-chain making was 'an industry which still remains practically a British monopoly'. The year was 1908 and an advertisement appeared in the *Newcastle Chronicle* saying that 'chain smiths were required at a works on the banks of the Rhine'. The news quickly filtered down to Staffordshire. What they advertised for were the services of two cable-chain makers together with their four strikers. I spoke about this to Bob Denholm of Dudley Wood, who was employed at Noah Hingley, as were his father and grandfather before him, and he told me that the men who were interested had worked at Hingleys. One of the men was contemplating leaving and had already 'obtained a situation at a works in Old Hill'. A representative of the firm from Duisburg, and an interpreter, duly arrived at the Hingley works and eventually six men consented to go to Germany. Bob Denholm described the situation in chain-makers' terms: 'Two or three fires went to Germany' – 'fire' being the term for the group of chain-makers who normally worked as a team around a hearth.

The officials of the Chain Makers' and Strikers' Union obviously did not like the

it seems to have been regarded as quite an important one. The printing on its certificates was jet black, and certainly stood out among the other coloured ones reproduced in the book.

Some other print colours shown on the proving house certificates were as follows:

Lloyds Proving House, Tipton:	blue
Lloyds Proving House, Low Walker:	red
Lloyds Proving House, Chester (Saltney):	mauve or pale purple
Lloyds Proving House, Cardiff:	brown
Lloyds Proving House, Glasgow:	green
River Wear Commission:	blue

The certificates also recorded the marks stamped on to the chain or anchors to show where they had been tested; for example, Lloyds Proving House, Chester, used the letters LPH-C, while Glasgow stamped LPH-G.

idea of the knowledge and skills that had been built up over many years in England by its chain-makers being passed on to foreign chain-makers, which would then allow them to compete with Britain for the chain business. The secretary of the union, Tom Sitch, and a representative from Noah Hingley went out to Germany to look into the situation. They found out that the men were kept under observation at all times and even they had difficulty in communicating with them. Sitch did not have much success at first but a little later the men wrote home to say that they were willing to come back to England if their 'release' could be arranged. Well-organised secret arrangements were made and a note was passed to them asking them to be at the local railway station at a certain time. The men were spirited away and returned to the Black Country to carry on their trade.

Their stay in Germany was not without incident. One of the men, described by Denholm as 'a bit of a character', did not like what he thought was the German locals in the pub talking about them in their native tongue, 'thame bxxxxx torkin about us agen' he would say, and would then wade into groups of three or four of them with his fists flailing. He was deported from Germany as a trouble-maker and another man went over to take his place. A few years later this same man found himself back in Germany, this time with the Army, in which he had risen to the rank of sergeant-major. After the end of the First World War he returned to Hingleys to carry on producing chain in the forge.

An example of the information contained on a test certificate can be seen in the illustration on page 93.

By law a link in every 5 fathoms had to be marked. It was usual to select the end links and also two common links near the middle of the 15-fathom length for this purpose.

Lloyds of Netherton Test House, Halesowen Road, Netherton, on the side of the Dudley No. 2 Canal, was the last proving house to close down in the country (in 2005 the buildings still existed, having been put to good use by a steel stockholder). The other ones in the Black Country area were all closed by the late 1960s or early 1970s. One possible reason for the Netherton proving house being the longest-lasting may be found in a handbook in my possession entitled *Regulations and Price List*, issued by Lloyds British Testing Company in August 1929, which gives a list of the Testing Establishments throughout the country. Under each proving house is shown the amount to which each of its machines could subject a length of chain or an anchor to test, either 'breaking' or 'tensile'. The Netherton house leads the table with a machine that can carry out a breaking test up to 400 tons and a tensile test up to 250 tons. Tipton, the Cambrian Proving House at Saltney and the Tyne Proving House at Low Walker all had machines capable of breaking tests up to 250 tons and tensile tests up to 150 tons. Kinning Park in Glasgow could break up to 180 tons and tensile test up to 130 tons while the proving houses at Cradley Heath (still standing in 2005) and Sunderland could break up to 150 tons and tensile test up to 107 and 101.5 tons respectively. Each testing establishment had between three and five testing machines that were licensed by the Board of Trade, under the Anchors and Chain Cables Act, 1899.

It is interesting to note that the *Journal of the Iron & Steel Industries* of 1902 carries a report on a discussion, which followed a paper read by E. von Halle on 'Chain Manufacture in Germany' before the German Naval Architects' Association. R. Rosenstiel discussed the reasons why the German chain-making industry had not succeeded in meeting the requirements for anchors and chains of the chief German shipping companies. He went on to say:

> Anchor chains are such important things that the ships' captains must have perfect trust in those supplied, and this trust they do not give to German chains, which are not publicly tested by an independent authority as in the United Kingdom. . . .
>
> German firms undoubtedly produce such chains of excellent quality, at least equal to the best English makes, if indeed they are not of still better quality. . . . All the anchors and chains that are required for the German Imperial Navy are made in Germany, and that these have given perfect satisfaction. They are submitted to the strictest tests at the Imperial Dockyards before being accepted, just such an independent test, that is, as Rosenstiel suggests for trading vessels, like that at Lloyds Proving House at Netherton. The question as to the possibility of establishing at present such a public testing institution in Germany and keeping it adequately employed is discussed and not considered practicable with the present condition of trade in Germany.

I thought that it was worth quoting that reference because it shows how well advanced the testing of chain was in the United Kingdom at that time and also the world-wide reputation already gained by Lloyds Proving House at Netherton. I have read in recent years that the Netherton Test House was regarded as the leading test establishment of the Lloyds group.

Today manufacturers of large cable-chain have their own test beds, and when chain is ready for test one of Lloyds' inspectors attends the works and supervises the test.

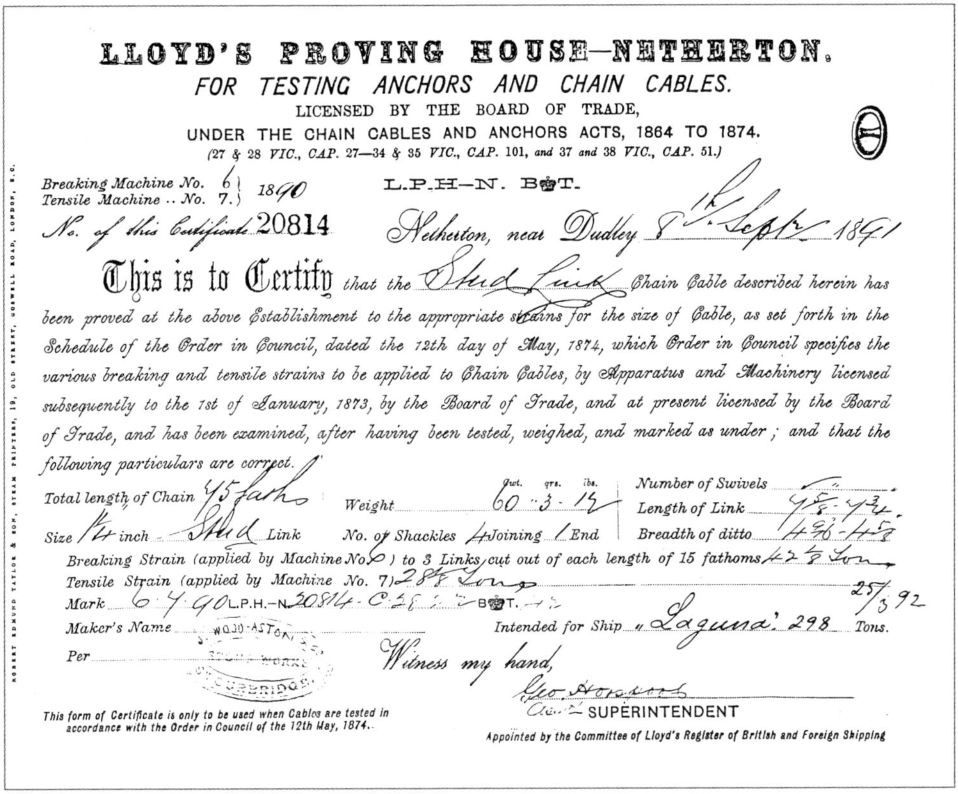

LLOYD'S PROVING HOUSE—NETHERTON.
FOR TESTING ANCHORS AND CHAIN CABLES.
LICENSED BY THE BOARD OF TRADE,
UNDER THE CHAIN CABLES AND ANCHORS ACTS, 1864 TO 1874.
(27 & 28 VIC., CAP. 27—34 & 35 VIC., CAP. 101, and 37 and 38 VIC., CAP. 51.)

Breaking Machine No. 6 } 1890
Tensile Machine .. No. 7. }
L.P.H—N. B♔T.

No. of this Certificate 20814 Netherton, near Dudley 8th Sept 1891

This is to Certify that the Stud Link Chain Cable described herein has been proved at the above Establishment to the appropriate strains for the size of Cable, as set forth in the Schedule of the Order in Council, dated the 12th day of May, 1874, which Order in Council specifies the various breaking and tensile strains to be applied to Chain Cables, by Apparatus and Machinery licensed subsequently to the 1st of January, 1873, by the Board of Trade, and at present licensed by the Board of Trade, and has been examined, after having been tested, weighed, and marked as under; and that the following particulars are correct.

Total length of Chain 45 faths — Weight cwt. qrs. lbs. 60 . 3 . 12 — Number of Swivels —
Size 1¼ inch Stud Link — No. of Shackles 4 Joining 1 End — Length of Link 7⅝–7¾ — Breadth of ditto 4⅝–4⅝

Breaking Strain (applied by Machine No. 6) to 3 Links, cut out of each length of 15 fathoms 42 ½ Tons
Tensile Strain (applied by Machine No. 7) 28 ⅞ Tons
Mark 6 · 7 · 90 L.P.H.—N. 20814 · C 28 ⅞ B♔T. 42 — 25/3 92
Maker's Name — Intended for Ship "Laguna" 298 Tons.
Per

Witness my hand,
Geo. Hopkins
Asst. SUPERINTENDENT
Appointed by the Committee of Lloyd's Register of British and Foreign Shipping

This form of Certificate is only to be used when Cables are tested in accordance with the Order in Council of the 12th May, 1874.

ROBERT EDMUND TAYLOR & SON, STEAM PRINTERS, 19, OLD STREET, GOSWELL ROAD, LONDON, E.C.

A typical Netherton test certificate.

Standardisation

The chain-making trade together with the associated manufacturing branches of anchor, shackle and other fittings was probably the first combined industry to adopt standardisation of sizes and test loads, as far back as 1858. This was mainly because Lloyds of London had to arrange insurance cover for ship owners and other companies involved and so was in a position to stipulate important standards of work, which were constantly improved and updated to suit ever-changing conditions.

Although Royal Navy anchor chain was originally ordered and supplied in lengths of 12½ fathoms, the most common length that was produced was 15 fathoms (90ft) long. The Navy also changed to this length in later years. The Navy originally specified 12½ fathom lengths because 8 lengths would then equal 100 fathoms which then equalled one 'cable', a seaman's measurement, of approximately one-tenth of a nautical mile.

The reason for settling on the 15-fathom measurement was that, under the rules of Lloyds Register, all anchor (or cable) chain had to be tested or Lloyds

Interior shot of the Lloyds test shop in Netherton. The men in the recess on the left are checking chain that has just been tested. The protective cover is in place on the next groove. The metal tubes on the right running up to the roof are taking fumes away from the joining hearths. Note the maximum daylight built into the shop.

would refuse to insure the ship. A length of 90ft was thought to be a reasonable one to handle and so test shops were built with enough clear space to test cables of this length.

The Navy also adopted the Lloyds rules for safety; in fact the Navy was sometimes even stricter in its specifications. The Navy always specified 'best best' wrought iron for its chains and steel for the studs in the chain while the mercantile marine was generally happy to abide by the Lloyds specification in the use of cast-iron studs in cable-chain.

Working to the 15-fathom length was also required by the various British chain standards, one of which specified that chain-testing machines 'shall not be used for loading more than 15 fathoms (90ft) in one test' and that 'The straining mechanism of the testing machine shall be sufficiently long to allow a chain of the full length of the test bed to be subjected to the proof load without the necessity for taking fresh hold to complete the strain.'

Each 15-fathom length of cable-chain supplied to a ship was made up of a number of 'common links', which was the nominal size of the chain specified (this was also the diameter of the bar of iron or steel that the links of chain were made from). This bar size was also the basis of a formula that controlled the length, breadth and radii of the three sizes of links that were required to make up the 15-fathom length of chain, and also the dimensions of the joining shackle supplied with it for connecting to the next 15-fathom length. Although BS3006:1949 specifies the limits to work to, which are necessary for any production job, the general formula for common links is for the overall length to be 6 times the diameter of the bar (for example the limits given in the tables are 6.0 to 6.15 times), the overall width to be 3.6 times the diameter of the bar and the inside radius of the link to be .58 of the size of the bar.

The bar of metal was normally round so as to cause as little friction as possible when links are working together but some examples were made out of square-section iron. At Wortley Top Forge links were made so that the contact between links was the point or corner of the square iron so that friction was reduced to the one point of contact. Large ground-mooring chain was also made of square iron. There must always be an odd number of 'common links' in a length of chain. This allows each end link to lie flat to facilitate connecting.

On each end of the common links is fitted an 'enlarged link', referred to in some manufacturers' lists (for example Henry Wood's list of 1916) as an 'intermediate link', which is an excellent name for a link that is between the common links and the end link, also sometimes called a joiner (the Black Country chain-maker called it a 'jine-er'). The enlarged link, as the name implies, was always made of metal slightly larger than the common links. BS3006 specifies a size which is 'seventeen-sixteenths times the nominal diameter of the common link in the length'. The length and breadth are then calculated by the same formula as before. Although the enlarged or intermediate link is fitted with a stud, the end link is left as an open link. This is again made of slightly larger metal, being specified as 1.2 times the size of the common link, and its overall size formula is also different, being length 6.75–6.9 times the bar size of the link, and the width 4.1–4.3 times. Not all printed lists agree with BS3006.

A few examples of the correct diameter size of 'enlarged' and 'end links' to be used with the common chain-links are as follows:

Common link	*Enlarged*	*End link*
$\frac{1}{2}$in	$\frac{9}{16}$in	$\frac{5}{8}$in
1in	$1\frac{1}{16}$in	$1\frac{3}{16}$in
2in	$2\frac{1}{8}$in	$2\frac{3}{8}$in
3in	$3\frac{3}{16}$in	$3\frac{5}{8}$in
4in	$4\frac{1}{4}$in	$4\frac{13}{16}$in

Obviously the standard 15-fathom lengths of chain had to be joined together to make various lengths of cable varying from 100ft to perhaps 300ft long. The first thing that was used, and is still used today, was a joining shackle. This is sometimes referred to as a 'bolt-type shackle' or a 'dee-type shackle'. Because a shackle is not such a geometrically strong form as a chain-link the metal that is used to make it must be of a larger cross-section than the common links of the cable-chain. The dimensions necessary are laid down by Lloyds Register and specified in BS3006:1949.

The overall length of a cable-chain link of course varies according to the diameter of the rod that it is being made from. To take two extreme examples, for $\frac{1}{2}$in diameter chain, the link is 3in long, while a 4in diameter chain-link comes out at 24in long. BS3006:1949 lists the dimensions of links from $\frac{7}{16}$in diameter (BS242) up to $4\frac{1}{2}$in (BS177), increasing by $\frac{1}{16}$in increments.

The same British Standards also specify such things as the minimum and maximum length over 10 common links, the minimum pitch of the common links (the measurement from the front of one link to the front of the next link standing on the same plane, that is the next but one in the chain), the minimum pitch from enlarged link and so on. All these measurements must be in tolerance 'after the statutory proof load has been applied'. This takes into account the fact that a length of chain settles and beds down and stretches while it is on the test bed. When the proof load test is carried out on a newly welded length of chain, a considerable amount of permanent stretch is noted. If the proof load is again applied to this same length of chain there should be no further elongation. This is one way that a chain-tester can tell if this piece of chain has been tested before.

There is, however, an exception to this rule. After a period of service a length of chain becomes 'work-hardened' and to return it to its former specification it is sometimes annealed or normalised by heating and cooling. This tends to soften the metal and so if it is put on test it will stretch again. If this process is repeated, the chain will stretch a little each time but not enough to interfere with its performance. By the time this procedure interferes with the working of the chain, it will be probably be worn out anyway.

A good action shot of a four-man team using a johnny two-handled hammer to finish off a join in a side-welded chain-link. The smith, the leader of the team, holds the tongs and the hollow tool that they are striking. The photograph was probably taken at the Henry Wood Works, near Chester, originally established at the Lye in the Black Country.

The Strength of a Chain-Link

The strength of a chain-link and its ability to carry out the job that it has been specified for depend upon a number of important factors: the form of the length and breadth; the diameter of the metal (obviously as the diameter of the metal increases so the strength of the link rises in proportion to it, and this also controls the standard dimensions); the properties of the material (a good-quality wrought iron was the preferred metal, having high anti-corrosive and good fire-welding qualities, with good strength and ductility); and last but not least in the case of a fire-welded wrought-iron or steel chain the skill of the chain-smith to make a sound join, weld or connection of the two ends of the formed bar which, if correctly carried out, will be as strong if not stronger than the rest of the metal in the link when finished.

First among these factors is the chain's form and size. The strongest type of chain-link is known as short link. As its name implies it is made to the smallest size that is possible for the diameter of the rod used in its manufacture while allowing easy and flexible movement of the links. The clearance between the links is kept to a minimum by using a straightforward formula: 'The outside overall length shall be equal to four and a half times the diameter of the rod and its outside width equal to three and a quarter times the size of the rod used.' This allows for a clearance of half the size of the diameter of the rod for movement inside the length of the link while the two adjoining links get an allowance of a quarter of the size of the rod for the working clearance inside the width of the link. Working strictly to this formula produces the strongest possible form of chain-link that can be made; any deviation from it makes the link progressively weaker. As the clearance between the links increases, the strength of the length of chain weakens.

Henry Wood of Chester listed in his 1916 catalogue a form of chain called 'Wood's Special Crane Chain'. This was described as being 'Made by selected workmen, from our special brand of iron, and made specially short in the

Terry Meecham of Lloyds (Brierley Hill) holding a three-link sample of 50mm (2in) Grade U1 steel chain that had already passed the proof load, or tensile test of 70 tonnes (twice the safe working load), and also the breaking load of 100 tonnes. It was then put on a short bed to be tested until it broke. The dial on the machine reached 210 tonnes before a link finally parted. As can be seen, even then it did not break on the side where the link was welded but in the crown of the link. *(Ron Moss)*

link.' The tolerances for this could have been even tighter than the standard formula, which is covered by BS394:1951. Wood's catalogue also listed various forms of open-link chain (this is chain that has no centre stud fitted), which are identified by the outside length, this allowing more working freedom in the centre of the link. They list a 'Short link or Rubble chain' having an outside length of '5 diameters of iron', a 'Middle link' having a length of 5½ diameters of iron, and an 'Open link' 6 diameters long.

Studs

Shortly after iron cable-chain replaced hemp rope for anchoring ships, which was from around 1808, it was soon realised that ordinary open-link chain, which was originally used, could get 'knotted-up' and if this happened when the anchor was being run out, and a knotted section tried to pass through the 'hawse-hole', the anchor chain would either jam, or if a heavy anchor was being dropped it could easily take out part of the side of the ship. To prevent this, from 1813 onwards a cast-iron (or later steel) waisted stud was inserted across the centre of the chain-link. This allowed for free movement of the chain but kept apart both of the links that were working inside each link of chain and also prevented the sides of the link from closing in when a heavy strain came upon the cable, for example when a ship was at anchor and riding out a heavy storm.

One of the qualities of chain is that it is a strong but very flexible metal connection. If an excessive strain is put on a length of chain, and it has been properly manufactured, it will stretch and close up until one side of the link is almost touching the other one. This action converts what is meant to be a flexible connection into a virtually solid piece of iron or steel or one, as most chain-makers say, 'like a walking stick'. If and when this happens, the chain will be useless as a flexible connection. This is one reason why studded cable-chain will not stand such a large tensile load on the test bed as open-link chain of the same diameter, simply because it is not allowed the inward movement when the load is applied. It will break under test before the test load of open-link chain is reached.

This important improvement in cable-chain technology is generally credited to Thomas Brunton and sometimes Captain Samuel Brown. Thomas Traill tells us the following. In 1813 Thomas Brunton, who is described as a merchant living in Cooper's Row, Crutched Friars, London, obtained a patent for certain improvements in the manufacture of certain articles, one of them being cable-chain. The patent was obtained in March and enrolled in September 1813. The improvement that concerns us was the fitting of his (Brunton's) broad-ended stay (stud). The patent said: 'The stay was to be put in while the link was red hot and the sides of the link closed by a die or press or in any other way. . . .'

The design of the stud, and the method of inserting it, has not changed to this day. Brunton's patent was afterwards declared void by three judges, but it is said that had he only claimed for his broad-ended stud it would have been upheld. On obtaining his patent he commenced manufacturing cable-chains, and soon established a good business.

Samuel Brown stated later that he was the first to begin fitting the stud. He certainly advocated the fitting of studs, both pointed and broad types, some time after Brunton's patent but in twisted chain-links. One critic said that the pointed stud tended to act as a chisel to cut through the side of the link and so rupture it, and the twist in the chain soon pulled out when under strain. Certainly Brown's idea of twisted links with pointed studs did not catch on.

Also in 1813 the firm of William Hawks & Co., of Gateshead-on-Tyne, commenced making stud-link chains. Brunton instituted a law suit against Hawks for an infringement of his patent of 1813, and this was decided in Brunton's favour. There was an appeal and it was decided that the patent was wholly void, and that there might be a new trial. Later Hawks manufactured stud-cables under an agreement with the patentee and a new trial was not necessary. So I think that we can safely say that Brunton can duly be credited with the idea of fitting studs.

Most chain-studs or stay-pins are made of cast iron. This common, basic form of iron, containing a fair amount of carbon, is hard and brittle but also has the property of being strong in compression and is admirably suited for the task of keeping the two sides of a chain-link apart. The Admiralty, however, usually specified in its contracts that the studs fitted to cable-chain made for the Navy must be of steel. An Admiralty tender that I saw that was to run from 13 May 1803 to 31 December 1807 specified that 'The stay-pins in its cable [chain] shall be either of forged or annealed crucible cast steel.' It also specified that 'All the stay-pins of the cable shall be marked on one side with the name or initials of the contractors, and on the other side with the date of the year of delivery into store. . . .'

The size of the stud increases with the size of the chain-link and sometimes has a raised number cast on it on the outer side to identify it. I have yet to see a table that specifies what number is to be used with a particular size of chain-link, or even if different firms had their own code for identifying different sizes of stud. Sometimes larger firms had their names cast on to the other side of the stud in raised letters; this told the world that they were proud of their products and also acted as an advert. One such firm was Noah Hingley of Netherton. An example that I have in my collection contains the name

'HINGLEY' on one side of the stud and the number 16 on the other. By checking the size, it appears to be for fitting into a $2\frac{1}{4}$in diameter cable-chain-link; how the number 16 relates to its size I have yet to discover. The outer ends of studs are cast with an inside radius that must match the diameter of the material that the chain is made from. By measuring across the widest part of the inside radius of a stud one can tell the size of cable-chain it should be used for.

A hollow recess allows the stud to locate nicely in the centre of the link when its sides are closed in on it, at the end of the manufacturing process while the link is still hot. It is not welded in position or physically joined to the outer link.

Studs are also curved on their sides, which is sometimes referred to as being 'waisted'. Some firms on occasion fitted studs which had quite narrow waists and were referred to as 'female studs'.

I was told by a Black Country chain-maker that some of the finest studs available were cast by the firm of John Barnsley & Sons, which was situated at the junction of Saltwells and Cradley Road, near Netherton. It was said that their studs were cast in brass moulds, and when they stopped making them and moved premises to Overend Road, Cradley Heath, some time around the 1960s, the moulds were collected by a 'tatter' (a wandering scrap dealer). Perhaps the idea of using brass moulds came about from the experience gained by John Barnsley & Sons (established in the year 1808) with another product – the company became world famous for producing 'jaws harps' (often wrongly referred to as 'jews harps'), which are played by holding the instrument against the teeth, and 'twanging the spring'. Barnsley's 20 August 1814 price list (priced 'per gross') correctly describes them as 'jaws harps'. Barnsley & Sons carried on production of seven different types of jaws harps for around a hundred years.

The specification for the centre-studded link in the anchor attachments that were made for the White Star Line liners *Olympic* and *Titanic* called for a steel stud in their $5\frac{1}{2}$in diameter links. The four-link anchor attachment made at Noah Hingley of Netherton for the *Lusitania* had steel studs made in two halves that were riveted together, when in position in the link, with five rivets. The attachments consisted of three $5\frac{1}{2}$in diameter links, with the one next to the anchor shackle being $5\frac{3}{4}$in diameter. The weight of the four links alone came to 16cwt 3qr 7lb and the team of smiths that made them are recorded as being paid 20*s* per hundredweight, which of course was then shared between the members of the gang.

Some firms took the trouble to have their name cast on their chain-studs, which once helped underwater archaeologists to identify the manufacturer of some cable-chain that was lifted from a wreck found off the remote Shetland Island of Foula in 1973–8.

I was most interested to have my attention drawn to a letter received by Geoffrey Hingley, managing director of the old chain-making firm of Barzillai Hingley and Sons (established 1815). The letter came from Simon Martin, of the salvage firm of Crawford and Martin, in December 1978. The firm had, for the previous five years, been carrying out the salvage of bearings, propellers and other items from the White Star liner *Oceanic*, which had been wrecked in 1914. It noted that the cable-chain, which had 'been rumbling about on the shallow reef for more than 60 years' was in remarkably fine condition. The studs in the links bore the name 'HINGLEY' and as Foula was in 'a wild spot' Crawford and Martin had to make plans at the end of each summer to lay their own heavy moorings so that their salvage ship could ride out the rough seas through the winter months. They retrieved some of the *Oceanic* anchor chain and 'Our salvage boat lay quite happily on the nineteenth-century Hingley chain.' I corresponded with Mr Martin: apparently they had scanned through the then current list of chain manufacturers and the only Hingley remaining in business was Barzillai Hingley and Sons; Noah Hingley had by this time changed name to Wright, Hingley, and as the company no longer made chain it was not listed as a chain-maker.

Geoffrey Hingley told Martin that the probable manufacturer of the *Oceanic* chain was Noah Hingley, adding that the size of the chain 'was far bigger than any that we ever made'. This is confirmed by an article in *Navy and Army Illustrated* of 11 February 1899 which tells us that 'They [N. Hingley & Sons] have just turned out the anchors and cables for the monster White Star liner, the *Oceanic*, which has recently been launched. Her anchors each weigh 7¼ tons, and her iron cables are 3¼in in diameter. Hingley roll their own iron for chain-cables, and have long been noted for their first rate work.' Noah Hingley in fact made the first cable-chain in the area in 1820; it was 1½in diameter and it was the first cable-chain in the Midlands to be fitted with studs.

The teams of men who made the large side-welded chain in the larger works such as Noah Hingley & Sons of Netherton, Henry Wood & Co. of Saltney, Brown, Lenox & Co. of Pontypridd, South Wales, to name just three of the pioneers of the chain industry, were a special breed of men, virtually a law unto themselves. The best description that I have read to date of these hard-working men was given by Mr Henry Woodhouse in his presentation *Historical Survey of the Chain Trade*, which was written in 1936 and revised in 1943. It is so brilliant that I feel I must reproduce it here in full.

A johnny-hammer in action shutting a large cable-chain link, having a team of three men to handle it.

> I scarcely need to tell you that chain-smiths are in a class by themselves, especially so the men we call 'Big Chain-makers', who in their unconventional dress or undress, are quite picturesque, big hefty men some of them are, and their scorn for buttons and braces is only equalled by their courage.
>
> Everything is anchored to a belt or strap at what appears to be perilously low altitude, but they know no fear, and are equally frank and outspoken.
>
> There is no difficulty in calling a spade a spade, but while their speech is plain of a kind it is decorative and might even be said to be colourful.
>
> These men are just as free in other ways; ordinary factory discipline simply does not apply. They have their own code of hours which is accepted by their employers as a matter of course.
>
> They start to work when they like, and stop when they like, and their day is often done by 11 or 12 o'clock, but in fairness I must say they could hardly do otherwise, as it is terribly hard work, and one would have to have a heart of stone who was not moved to compassion on seeing these men, especially in the heat of summer, saturated and soaked in sweat to their very boots.

Because of their terribly hot working conditions the big-chain makers traditionally started work very early in the morning, or more accurately, halfway through the night, to avoid the heat of the day. The few books that mention the chain trade usually repeat the statement that the chain-makers began their labours early in summertime when the temperatures were high and then reverted to later starting times during the cooler winter months. Over the years of research that I have carried out I have located and spoken to many 'side-welders', as the men who worked on the large chain were called, and most of them have told me that the very early start times were in fact maintained throughout the year. It was not uncommon for the side-welders and other forge-men who worked on large pieces such as shackles, rings and anchors to leave home at about 3.00 a.m. and, as no public transport was around at that time in the early morning, the majority would then walk to work so as to make a start in the forge at 4.00 a.m. or so. Some members of the crew would be there even earlier to get the forge and hearth fires going so that they would be ready for the smiths when they arrived. One old Noah Hingley side-welder told me that he started very early in the morning and was usually back home in time to take his children to school for 9.00 a.m.

This did mean that, after a lunchtime drink, a lot of them would have a nap in the afternoon and go to bed early in the evening so that they could be well rested and ready to start their heavy job again the next morning. As there were few residential districts in the Cradley, Cradley Heath, Old Hill and Netherton area that did not have domestic or brewhouse chain-shops in great profusion in their midst, it was not uncommon for the big-chain makers to be unable to get to sleep because of the tapping or hammering of the small-chain makers in the workshops quite literally below their bedroom windows. One inhabitant told me that a local by-law was introduced prohibiting the making of chain in domestic chain-shops after 9.00 p.m.

The Mrs Greenfield mentioned in the previous chapter would send her two sons to the corners of the street, when she had an urgent chain order to complete, with instructions that, should they see a policeman or a stranger in a suit approaching, they were to hurry back and tell her. She would then cover the barred windows with 'urden bags' (hessian bags) to hide the glow from her fire, and she would stop hammering until the coast was clear.

Mrs Pardoe, who was the landlady at The Swan, the famous home-brew public house in the High Street, Netherton, told us while the Black Country Society Industrial Archaeology Group was carrying out a survey of her brewery when the old 'copper boiler' was being taken out in the 1970s, that her pub was on the route of the chain-makers who walked to work at Noah Hingley, Netherton, from the direction of Dudley. Many of them would drop in early in the morning and 'have a whisky on the slate'. The cost of this tipple would be chalked on a piece of slate kept behind the bar. The men would pop in on pay day and settle the account, and of course have another.

Integral Stud Cable-Chain

The development of the integral stud-link cable-chain took place during the period 1942–3. In order to develop the new chain, two old established chain-making companies, William Griffin & Sons and Woodhouse Brothers, joined together to form the new firm, Griffin-Woodhouse. The Admiralty was of course very interested in this development and, being in the middle of a world war in which cable-chain was very much in demand for ships, it stepped in and provided much-needed support to help in its development. One account of the history of Griffin-Woodhouse that I have read stated that the Navy actually took over the firm to control the manufacture of the integral chain for the duration of the war, and handed it back to the previous management once hostilities had ceased.

The idea of forging the stud on to the bar of steel before it was bent into the oval shape of the link is said to have originated with a Jack Timmington. Many of the local chain-making firms who at that time were making cable-chain by hand, were being supplied with rods of rolled wrought iron by

One of the early stages of producing integral stud-link chain. This fortunate shot in the yard of the Griffin-Woodhouse Works near Cradley Heath railway station shows the stud already forged on to the bar before it is reheated and bent into a link. No way will this stud now leave the link even in typhoon conditions.

Ratcliffes Rolling Mills of Oldbury. One version of the story of how the idea of the integral-stud chain emerged was that one of the lorries delivering supplies of iron to the yard had a registration number that ended in '999'. If one imagined that the centre of the figure 9 was the cable-chain stud, then all that was required was to extend the numeral's 'tail' back up to join the centre and hey presto, a chain-link had been created that contained a stud that was permanently attached to one side of the link and could not work loose or drop out when in service in heavy seas.

Walter Guest of Samuel Woodhouse & Sons, Corngreaves, Cradley Heath, is said to have been involved with the idea in its early days, but the critical development and tool and die design was masterminded by Harry Stevens of Old Hill, working at that time for Griffin-Woodhouse.

The first part of the manufacture was to upset-forge the end of the rod of steel so as to provide enough metal at right angles to the side in order to allow the rod to be placed between dies to form the stud. This could be carried out while still hot from the first operation or after reheating a second time depending on how production was running or how large was the chain-link. Between these first operations, of course, as was normal practice in forging, the 'flash', or surplus metal, displaced by the die blocks was 'clipped off', or removed, and the rod cut to its correct length, which is quite critical. The stud was positioned almost at the end of the rod but a small part of the side member of the link was allowed to project. This was lined up with the other end and later electrically welded to it after the final reheating and bending operation brought these two ends together, so completing the oval link.

This is the only integral-stud chain that is manufactured to the registered patent and it is supplied to most of the world's shipping companies. The range of sizes available starts at $^{11}/_{16}$in diameter (this is the diameter of the rod from which it is initially manufactured) up to over $3^{1}/_{2}$in diameter (actually 93mm diameter), and it is available in various alloy steels to suit the customer's requirements. It is patented under the name of GWEC Integral Stud Link Chain Cable and in the 1990s it was still manufactured by Griffin-Woodhouse of Woods Lane, Cradley Heath, from a factory situated near Cradley Heath railway station.

Machine-Made Chain

For many, many years various iron-works and chain-works tried to mechanise the making of chain, particularly because the large side-welded (over 2in diameter) type is quite labour-intensive.

Here the integral stud-link chain has been formed into a link and awaits welding of the join on the side.

Here a small chain can be seen being welded on an automatic machine. The surplus pips of metal produced by the former that re-created the diameter of the chain after the welding operation can be seen on the right of the picture about to be sheared off.

An article appeared in *The Engineer* dated 26 October 1894 containing drawings of a machine developed by the engineering firm of Walzwerk Germania, based at Neuweld-on-the-Rhine. This consisted of a series of four rollers, each having the shape of a continuous chain formed in them. A cruciform bar was heated and fed through the rollers, which squeezed the shape of the chain on it. While still warm the formed bar was then passed through a punching machine, which removed the excess metal, or webs. The bar was then heated to red heat and pulled to its finished size, which also separated each link.

I found a similar process recorded as Patent 20,992 of 1897. This was credited to Alexander George Strathern of Hillside Stepps, County of Lanark, Engineer. It was manufactured from cruciform bar and used a series of punches and dies in slides. The machine was 'driven by large gears and a steam powered motor'. The patent noted that fins or burrs of metal would be left filling the spaces between the links. Another patent, No. 260,105 of 1926, dealt with the manufacture of chain-links and was also filed by Alexander George Strathern, who puts his address as '50 Wellington Street, Glasgow'.

My late friend Keith Gale made available to me a leaflet dealing with 'Weldless Steel Chains', the managing director of the company concerned being Alex. G. Strathern and the firm being based at Gartsherrie, Coatbridge, Scotland. This chain appeared to be rolled from a cruciform bar. The size range covered sizes from $\frac{1}{2}$in to $1\frac{1}{2}$in (diameter). Although no date was stated, Keith estimated that it was around the late 1920s or 1930s.

I have also found references to 'M. Rongier's method', as used at the Patent Weldless Chain Company in Aston, Birmingham. This also appears to have been made from a steel cruciform bar and covers smaller sizes from $\frac{1}{2}$in down to $\frac{3}{32}$in diameter. This reference was dated 1894.

Small-Chain

The smaller sizes of chain were the first to be successfully produced by machine. The development of the forming, or bending, machine and the process of electrically welding the steel chain-links is credited to M. Bosshard of France in 1901.

Samuel Woodhouse & Sons of Corngreaves Road, Cradley Heath, a chain-making firm founded in 1870, was the first to acquire the patent and introduce electrically welded chain into Great Britain in 1903. It took a few years to iron out the snags but soon the process was supplying the needs of all small-chain users. Even so, women were still making hand-made small-chain until the last one, Lucy Woodhall, finally retired, ironically from Samuel Woodhouse & Sons' Eagle Chain Works in December 1973. When I spoke to

Wilson Woodhouse, director of Samuel Woodhouse & Sons, in 1990 he said that the women's small-chain trade had of course been affected by the introduction of machine-made chain, but the outworking system in which many women made the small-chain in their own backyard chain-shops in the Cradley Heath district had flourished for 80 to 100 years and had only started to die off in about 1930. It was hit by the depression of the 1930s and the introduction of more tractors on the farms, which meant the end of demand for chain used on, or with, horses.

In the process of making electrically welded steel chain, two separate machines are used. The first one is a 'bending and lacing' machine. This is loaded with coiled steel 'wire' on to a revolving stand. A Holden & Hunt instruction book tells us that the coils should weigh about 1½cwt. I enquired about the weight of the coils delivered today and was told 'they are 200 kilos' (approximately 4cwt). The loaded wire is then pulled, or passed through straightening rollers and then cut off to the required length; this is called in the trade a 'plug'. It is then partly bent to the shape of the link by a pair of bending tools pushing the plug towards a very hard centre former, made of molybdenum steel. This forms the shape of the link apart from leaving a gap in the side so that the previously made link can be threaded through, and then the ends of the new link closed up. The length of formed chain then falls to the floor into a container, ready to be passed to the welding machine.

Holden & Hunt's instruction book recommends that, after bending and before welding, the length of chain should be lightly polished to clean it. Today the chain is cleaned ultrasonically, taking off the majority of the oil (which is always found on drawn rod and is a necessary lubricant used in the drawing process) and the dirt. The length of unwelded chain is then set up in the welding machine and usually every other link is welded at this stage, because it is most convenient for the link to be standing on its edge to facilitate the welding process.

In July 1991 I recorded the sequence of welding a link on a Meyer Roth & Pastor machine. This was in regular use at the factory of Joseph Woodhouse (Chains), Foxoak Street, Cradley Heath. It was fortunate that I was able to pay this visit just before the works was closed and the machinery was moved to the Mushroom Green works of Griffiths Chains. The Woodhouse works buildings have now been demolished.

The machine operator stood in front of these machines and more or less kept an eye on the welding of the chain. The two end faces to be welded were squeezed together lightly and the pressure was maintained by a system of rods and four large coil springs about 8in long, very similar to garden gate springs. These could be seen below the 'welding area' in the front of the machine.

A good illustration of the welding of the machine-made link on the carousel chain-making process used at Lloyds Chain Works, Brierley Hill. This was once the home of the Samuel Taylor Chain and Anchor Works. *(Terry Meecham)*

Two copper electrodes positioned themselves one on each side of the gap in the link and the electric current (2–3 volts, 60–80 amps) heated up the link metal. As the metal softened the pressure from the large springs underneath caused the two faces to come together and so fused the two ends. While the metal was still hot and pliable two forming tools moved in to deal with the excess metal that had been generated by the welding process. These two tools moved to the front and the back of the link and each of them had the internal radius form of half the diameter of the chain being made. This operation squeezed the excess metal back to the correct diameter; any excess metal was left as two 'fins' at the top and bottom of the link. As the length of chain moved on down a V-groove on the right-hand side of the machine, a pair of cutting tools automatically moved across and cut off the two fins.

The chain would then be set up again so that the alternate links could also be welded. Sometimes another similar welding machine was set up next to the first one and the chain immediately fed from one machine to the next to weld the alternate link. However, Geoffrey Woodhouse of Joseph Woodhouse

This 26mm (1in) cable-chain has been developed by Lloyds (Brierley Hill), a former member company of the Triplex Group, for use on Royal Navy mine-hunter vessels. It is made from silicon-aluminium-bronze alloy to satisfy the non-magnetic specifications for equipment for these ships. The alloy and joining weld are so strong that they are able to pass the Lloyds-specified tensile tests as carried out on steel chain of the same dimensions. *(Photograph by Ron Moss, reproduced by kind permission of Lloyds (Brierley Hill) Ltd)*

(Chains) said to me that he preferred to pass the length of chain back through the original machine so that it would be uniform throughout its length.

Large Cable-Chain

Experimental work on machine-making larger cable-chain was carried out between 1907 and 1910 in the Sheffield District and also by the British Machine Made Cable Co. at Netherton. This gave promising results and regulations for testing were issued, but commercial success did not follow.

The British Machine Made Cable Co. was a company set up for making machine chain by Noah Hingley of Netherton. Information was passed on to me by old Hingley chain-makers that Harland & Wolff, the ship-builders of Belfast, who at that time had under construction the White Star liners *Titanic* and *Olympic,* heard of the experiments with the new steel machine-made chain and thought that it would be appropriate to have this modern chain on these luxury ships and so placed the order with Noah Hingley of Netherton.

Because it would be a few more years before all the manufacturing problems with machine-made chain had been ironed out, even though Noah Hingley indeed supplied the cable-chain and anchors for these great ships, all of it was made by hand. Fortunately several photographs recording the making and despatch of this chain and anchor order were saved, together with the order books.

Tayco Chain

Another revolutionary steel machine-made cable-chain designed and made in the Black Country and supplied to famous 1930s liners was Tayco chain. Samuel Taylor & Sons (Brierley Hill) started experimenting to produce a machine-made cable-chain in 1915. It was 1931 before the company was satisfied enough with the finished product and supplied the first length of this new cable-chain, which was made to the order of the Admiralty. In the same year the chain was approved by Lloyds Register and the Board of Trade. The links of this chain were drop-forged in dies, complete with cross-studs from plain carbon-steel billets which, for merchant ships, had an ultimate tensile strength of 35 tons per square inch. For the Admiralty, steel of a somewhat higher tensile strength was used.

The patent specification was No. 433,660 and it was filed by the Samuel Taylor managing director Humphrey J. Taylor, the complete specification being accepted on 19 August 1935. During the Second World War various local drop-forging firms made this chain under licence for the Admiralty. I have a copy of one of the drawings giving details of the links and containing a rubber stamp for the Smethwick Drop Forge at their Kidderminster Works. They made it under licence until around 1944. Production at Brierley Hill was discontinued in late 1969.

So that a continuous length of chain could be manufactured, every other link was made up in sections that were either forged as half-links or as complete links and sawn in half through the centre stud. The centre stud itself was then cut through and the half-link heated enough so that the centre stud part could be opened up and a complete forged chain-link passed through it and the gap closed up. It was then temporarily joined to a matching half-link using special sheet-steel metal hooks and the length of chain passed to the welding machine. The half-links to be welded were clamped into heavy copper jaws so that each half-link formed a terminal for the electrical circuit. The faces of the two half-links were then brought together and, with the electrical current on, because of the resistance resulting from the light contact, a rise in temperature would occur. When a sufficient temperature rise had been obtained the half-links were then separated, thus causing an arc.

Drop-forging the links for Tayco chain at the Samuel Taylor Works, Brierley Hill. The next operation will be to remove the thin metal remaining in the centre of the links.

Contact and separation were repeated until a welding heat was reached. The jaws holding the half-links were then mechanically forced together and the weld completed. Surplus metal was removed with pneumatic chippers and the chain was then heated and normalised. The largest Tayco welding machine had a capacity of 800kVA, 1,000 amps at 5–6 volts, and was capable of welding 5in diameter cable-chain.

Blaco Chain

Brown-Lenox of Pontypridd, whose chain-making record stretches back to the early nineteenth century, had a modern chain-making machine installed in about 1957. This was a Swedish Asea-Svets machine which had a continuous process for making the chain-link with the join in the link being electrically welded, and if cable-chain was required a centre stud could also be inserted as the last operation in the sequence. This chain appeared in

ne of the machining operations on Tayco chain-links that ensures a smooth location is made with the ext inserted link.

This photograph shows a steel link being formed before being electrically welded on a carousel machine at Lloyds (Brierley Hill). Chain has been made on this site for many years. The works were previously occupied by Samuel Taylor & Sons (Brierley Hill) who made their Tayco chain there. This chain was supplied to Cunard for use on the Queen liners. *(Photograph by Lloyds (Brierley Hill) Ltd)*

adverts described as Blaco chain, a name presumably conjured up from the initials of Brown-Lenox and Asea-Svets and Co.

The machine worked on the 'carousel' or 'roundabout' principle whereby the cut piece of high-tensile steel rod was placed in the first 'station' and heated electrically. It was then taken to the next station where it was bent into a U-shape and threaded though the last link made. The final bend was then made which closed the two ends together before it was passed on to another station where the two ends were electrically welded. The next operator then guided the freshly welded link into a vice or clamp and proceeded to trim off the excess weld with a pneumatic chisel. At the last station the operator inserted the stud, if required, and applied pressure to close the sides of the link on to the stud. As each operator finished his task he put his foot on a floor button and, when all the station buttons had been pressed, the inside turntable moved around to the next position. The lengths of finished chain then piled up on the centre turntable.

For the Brown-Lenox information I am grateful to P.F. Grove of Sturminster Newton who was involved with installation and the running of the plant in 1957–63.

The Noah Hingley company of Netherton experimented from 1915 onwards with electrically welded machine-made chain, but without too much success until around the time of the Second World War. A special company called the British Steel Chain Company was set up in Old Hill, a couple of miles from the Netherton Works. Hingleys also used the Asea-Svets machines successfully to produce electrically welded chain. The modern-looking works buildings and offices are still to be seen. In about 1966, with re-organisation of the many companies in the group and following a fire in

'ayco cable-chain, as fitted to the anchors of the P & O liner *Stratheden*.

the works, the machines and equipment were moved to the Samuel Taylor chain-works in Brierley Hill, the famous Tayco process being phased out there by late 1969.

The works and office buildings in Old Hill are still standing today and are used by other firms. The machines are still turning out beautiful cable-chain, which is used to equip many ships of the Royal Navy. This chain is still manufactured today in part of the old Samuel Taylor works just outside Brierley Hill, on the same site that produced the *Queen Mary* and *Queen Elizabeth* anchor chains before the Second World War. The firm, together with all the other firms in the Hingley group, was taken over by Lloyds, the famous steel firm of Wednesbury, and more recently by Triplex.

Today much of the chain that was once manufactured in the Black Country is manufactured either on the Continent or in the Far East and imported. It is left to our local museums to demonstrate how chain was once made by hand.

Lugless Chain-Joining Shackle or Kenter Shackle

To save all the trouble of manufacturing different size links for every length of chain, the 'lugless chain-joining shackle' was introduced and eventually approved by Lloyds. It is generally accepted that the first one that was introduced was by the German Borsig company under the name of the 'Kenter' shackle. This has become such a well-used name in the chain trade that even if an ordinary shackle is being used they still say that a 'Kenter' is being used though it might not strictly be of that design.

Obviously when the Kenter shackle was first introduced everybody wanted to jump on the bandwagon. Everyone 'invented' their own type of lugless shackle. These of course had to be approved by Lloyds Register and this only happened after rigorous testing. The original Kenter shackle is a very good design, having several good mechanical holding surfaces fitting together like a jigsaw, the whole assembly being held together with a tapered pin. A lump of lead usually seals the end of the pin in place.

Besides not requiring special links at the ends of each length, the Kenter has another more important advantage over the common shackle. As it is similar in shape to the common cable-link, it allows for a smooth passage over the windlass or winding gear when the anchor is being lowered or weighed. It is generally of the same diameter, the same overall length and almost the same width as the rest of the chain in the length. The width of the link is 4.1 units (the unit being equal to the metal diameter of the common links) as against the normal cable-chain width of 3.5 to 3.7 units.

Lugless shackles are also available for attaching the cable-chain to the anchor.

Chapter 4

Anchors and Anchor Making

Three important objects depicting the town's industrial history appear on the coat of arms of the Borough of Dudley, often referred to as the Capital of the Black Country, namely an anchor, a trilobite and a Davy lamp. The Davy lamp, of course, is to recall the wealth of coal that was mined locally; the trilobite became known as the 'Dudley locust' because it was found in the limestone deposits in the Wren's Nest area where the limestone was mined for use in several industries; and of course the anchor is present because, remarkably for an inland town so far from the sea, anchors and cable-chain were manufactured in great quantities and used on the high seas by many ships of all countries for many years.

Early anchors sometimes consisted merely of a wooden crook with a stone fastened to it. These are quite often referred to as 'killicks' or mooring stones and are still used even today by lake fishermen. One theory is that the name 'anchor' came from the city on the banks of the River Nile in Egypt called Anchyronopolis, the city of anchors. Close by were quarries from where stone anchors were cut. Howard Carter found a miniature stone anchor shaped like a T-square, with one of the arms slightly pointed, fastened to one of the stern steering paddles of a boat of the 3,000-year-old funeral fleet of Tutankhamun.

The oldest iron anchor to be found was discovered when Lake Nemi in Italy was drained to ascertain the truth of the persistent tale that two Roman galleys belonging to the Emperor Caligula were lying on the bottom of the lake. The Italian Ministry of Public Instruction commenced emptying the lake in 1928 and in 1930 an iron anchor encased in wood was discovered. When the wooden sheathing was removed it was found to have a movable stock held in by a cotter-pin, and the pieces of iron forming the shape of the anchor, very similar to the early pattern of the Rodger's anchor patented in 1846, were beautifully welded together. The theory is that the wooden sheathing was added to give a better grip in the soft mud of the lake.

Forging Ships' Anchors

A good wine or whisky is often said to be at its best after it has matured or aged. During my research into iron working and forging I have come across many instances whereby ironmasters, involved in the manufacture of an article that must be right and last for a good length of time, performing its duties faultlessly, have decided to use pieces of iron that have already been worked on one job, iron that has aged and matured. All stress has been removed from this iron so that in its second working it can be relied upon to maintain its shape and form. Most anchor-makers therefore preferred to use pieces of old scrap iron when they were forging ships' anchors.

I have been told that, at the Noah Hingley works at Netherton, two men had the job of continually moving around the whole area with a wheelbarrow, collecting all the pieces of scrap iron that they could find. The off-cuts from jobs, especially the large pieces of round iron bar that were unusable when they were cut off at an angle for the making of side-welded chain (there would be at least two pieces from each bar), were eagerly collected. These scrap pieces were piled up, sometimes on top of a piece of wood (which of course would burn away in the furnace), banded or wired together, and placed in a 'ball furnace' to be heated up to the welding temperature of 1,300–1,400 degrees Centigrade, a light yellow colour, then taken out of the furnace and passed to the steam or helve hammer and hammer-welded into a slab or block. Another method was to 'box-pile' them, especially if the pieces were on the small side and difficult to band together. Flat pieces of iron plate were then used to form a box about 24in long by 6in wide and 6in deep into which the small bits of scrap iron were placed and the box was then finished off with another plate on top. This was then heated to welding heat and hammered into a block under a hammer. These blocks were then reheated and welded together until they were formed into a piece of iron that was large enough to make the shank or the arms of an anchor.

An article on 'Anchors & Chain Cables' by G. Lindsey that appeared in *British Manufacturing Industries* of 1878 described the process as putting together piles of scrap iron (preferred) weighing around 1½cwt each, which were then 'melted in a furnace' and placed under a steam hammer and hammered into slabs. The slabs were then placed together, fifty or a hundred at a time, according to the size of the anchor that was being made, and all joined or forged together. Sometimes iron bars were heated and forged together to form the larger pieces. Two references that I have found describe the use of lengths of wrought-iron rails, which became available as the various railway companies steadily replaced original iron track with rolled steel rails.

A proud team of early anchor forgers standing behind what is described as a 'common anchor'. They all appear to be wearing protective aprons made out of old hessian bags, known in the Black Country as urden bags.

When Prime Minister William Gladstone visited the chain and anchor works of Henry Wood & Co. at Saltney, near Chester (the Wood Brothers Chain and Anchor works had originally been established in The Lye, near Stourbridge, in 1780), the scene was described in the *Chester Chronicle* of 20 September 1890 as follows:

> The mass of iron, composed of double-headed rails, or railway iron called faggots, bunched together, to the weight of about a ton, was drawn out of the furnace, where it had been heating for about an hour and a half, and swung by an immense crane under the biggest steam hammer which quickly reduced its size, and brought it into shape.

Bob Denholm, a former forgeman and anchor smith at the Noah Hingley works, at Netherton, related to me a similar story: twelve to sixteen lengths of wrought-iron rail, each 10–12ft long and banded together, were put into a furnace where half of the bundle was heated to welding heat and hammered into a block, and the bundle was then swung around and the operation repeated on the other half. This method produced a large piece of very good iron that was ideal for forming the shank of an anchor.

The early stocked anchors used by the Navy at the beginning of the eighteenth century had a large wooden stock attached to the shank at the opposite end to the arms and above that a hole into which a ring was fitted so that the hemp cable and later the iron cable could be attached. The purpose of the stock, which was set at right angles to the arms and flukes or palms, was to turn the anchor on to a side when it hit the sea bottom so that the pointed flukes could then bury themselves into the sea bed and so hold the ship on station. Later an iron stock was substituted for the wooden one and then two holes were needed at the top of the shank, the top one to take a shackle, on to which the cable-chain was attached, and the second, larger, hole to take the iron stock. The stock was an iron rod, usually a little longer than the shank of the anchor and fitted with a 'ball-shape' on each end. One of the balls was removable and was usually held in position by a bolt so as to allow the stock to be removed from the shank. The stock was locked in its correct position in the shank by a flat taper-pin, which then located in a slot in the shank, the pin being attached to it by means of a short length of small-chain. The stock tended to cause problems when it was standing at right angles on the deck, especially when the Navy introduced the first turret guns, which fired across the decks of ships.

An alternative arrangement was introduced later whereby a 'bent-stock' was fitted. This allowed the stock to be passed through the hole in the shank, once the flat taper-pin was removed (in this arrangement the taper-pin was sometimes attached to the stock) and folded down to lie along the length of the shank without it actually being removed from the anchor for storage.

The two holes in the shank of the anchor were punched into the metal while still hot and under either a steam hammer, or before its introduction, using a 'beetle' hammer (which will be described later) or hand hammers, which would be the two-handled 'johnnies'. These varied in the weight of the head from 40 to 100lb. Also used was a three-handled 'Monday hammer' (which I have seen quoted as weighing up to 140lb), which actually needed as many as five men to handle it.

The shank was turned over and over as punches were used; these increased in size each time with the larger punch pushing out the previous smaller punch, as they tended to get trapped in the hot metal as they heated up themselves and of course the hole was cooling and closing up all the time. Finally the hole was made to the correct, finished size, remembering to allow

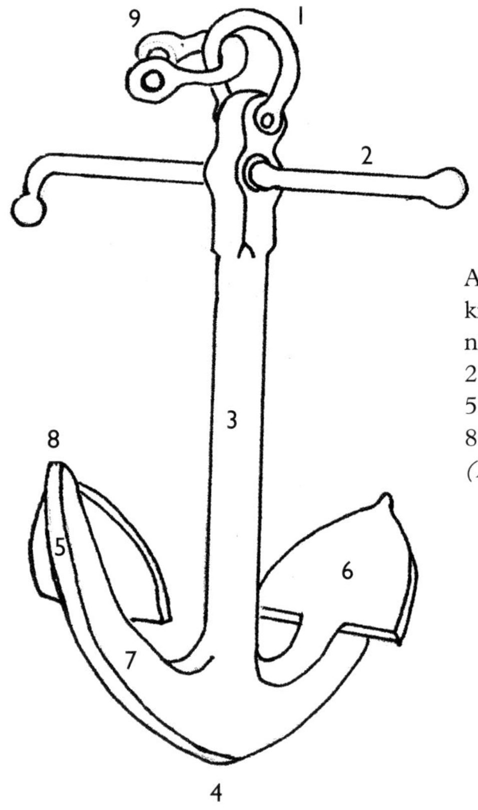

An iron stock anchor, sometimes known as a 'kedge' type. The named parts are: 1. Ring; 2. Stock; 3. Shank; 4. Crown; 5. Fluke; 6. Palm; 7. Arm; 8. Bill; 9. Shackle or Jaws harp. *(Ron Moss)*

for the cooling of the iron, which reduced the size of the hole. During this operation the shank was supported on 'bolsters' so as to give enough clearance to allow the punches used to drop out below.

Some anchors had only one arm and were called 'one-armed mooring anchors', while the familiar 'Emblem of Hope' or 'Admiralty mud-hook' had two arms. At the end of each arm was a point called either a 'fluke' or a 'palm', the shape of which varied according to whose anchor design it was. The 'Trotmans' or 'Porter Type' anchor was designed to allow the arms, which formed one part, to pivot in a slot in the bottom of the shank, enabling the anchor flukes to dig deep in the sea bed; these had quite complex flukes. These flukes have a right-angled design, with a projection known as a 'toggle', which helps the anchor to dig in. The flukes have to be fire-welded on to the arms before the arms are attached to the shank. If the anchor has one arm then a half-joint is used; this is very similar to the one used when working in wood by a carpenter. When the anchor has two arms, the shank has to have two reduced shoulders on to which the two arms are fire-welded using a much thinner half-joint (see the sketches on page 126).

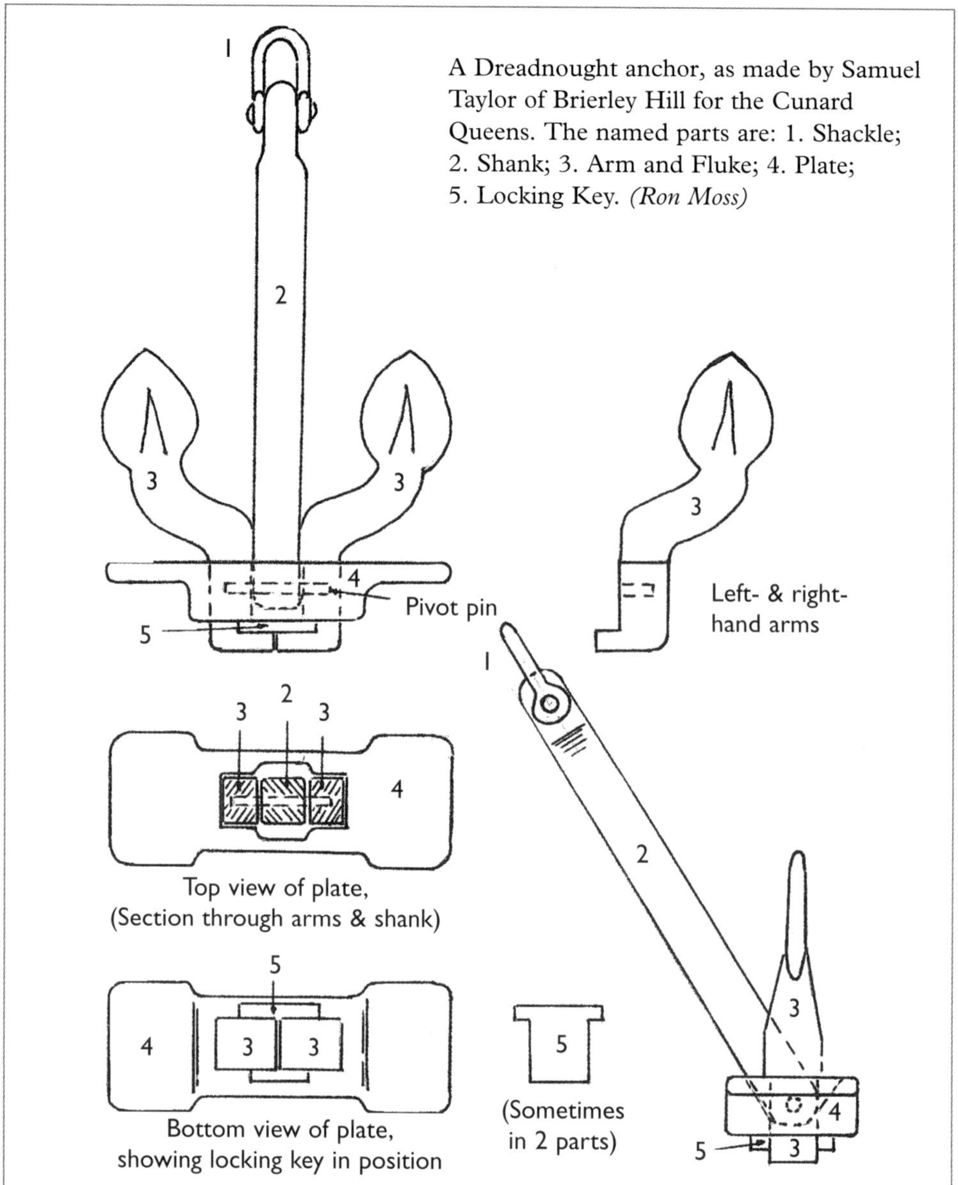

A Dreadnought anchor, as made by Samuel Taylor of Brierley Hill for the Cunard Queens. The named parts are: 1. Shackle; 2. Shank; 3. Arm and Fluke; 4. Plate; 5. Locking Key. *(Ron Moss)*

The operation of joining together the three main parts of an anchor was graphically described in the *Chester Chronicle* of 20 September 1890 by the reporter who covered Gladstone's visit to the Dee Ironworks of Henry Wood of Chester. The report described how the party of visitors made their way into a 'lofty shop' where big anchors were made (the company then had eight or nine anchor-shops) and where the anchor smiths had 'two great hearths glowing in front of two brick furnaces'. Presently they saw an immense shank drawn from the fire, which was some 14ft long; its end was white hot. This shank swung from a great crane and simultaneously there advanced towards it, also hanging from a crane, a pair of flukes of some 24cwt (the whole anchor would weigh about 55cwt). The reporter went on to say:

> This was a grand sight, the colour of the glowing metal being so beautiful . . . in fact, being a study of chromatics. Reaching forward came four men, two on each side with blazing bars of 'binding iron' with which to form the weld. Ten men rushed at the flaming mass with their hammers, and formed the junction with rapid swinging blows. Now there came down from the roof a long hammer alternately raised and lowered by two wheels or pulleys between which it played amongst the rafters above us [this would be a 'beetle', aforementioned]. This was used to cut off, with the aid of hand wedges, the projecting lumps of iron [these would be the remains of the bars of binding iron used; several feet were usually left 'sticking out on all points of the compass' – the extra feet were not only needed for ease of handling, but also to allow the anchor smith to stand well away from the terrific heat].

The reporter said that Gladstone watched the process with deepest interest, shading his face from the heat from time to time. One can appreciate that Gladstone and his party would be standing a distance away and so, if the heat affected him where he stood, one can imagine the heat given out and experienced by someone standing quite close to the mass of iron on which the anchor smiths were working. It was mentioned previously in the report that one of the ladies in the party 'drew back in alarm as the sparks flew out in showers, but was reassured'.

The weights given in that report do not amount to a very large anchor but Mr Coltart (of the Henry Wood firm) has explained to me that anchors of up to 7 tons in weight were forged in the works with one arm only, which was equal to an anchor of 9 tons with two arms. The 'bars of binding iron' mentioned in the report were bars of iron measuring around 1½in square that were used during the process of welding the anchor parts together and to fill up the gaps between each part. A special iron bar was rolled for filling in corners or larger joints and this was called 'glut iron'.

The anchor-shop had several hearths or fires around the sides, some large ones, in which the anchor parts to be joined together were heated up to welding heat, and a couple of hearths in which one or two dozen of these bars of binding iron would be coming up to welding heat at the same time as the anchor parts. While they were still hot, the unwanted parts of these bars would be cut off by means of one of the smiths holding a cutting-off wedge

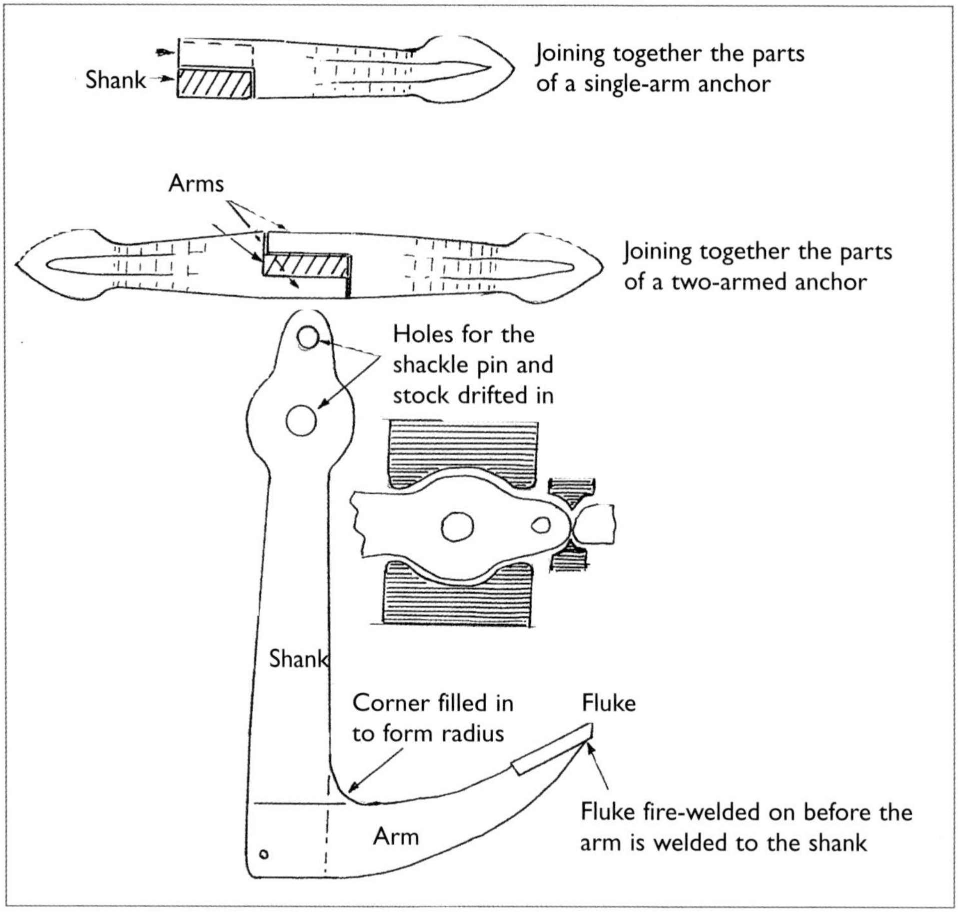

The making of an iron stock anchor. *(Ron Moss)*

while blows were rained down upon the back-end of the wedge using the beetle.

The beetle was a type of drop-hammer working on a similar principle to the old board-hammer. The main working part of it was a rod of iron, which measured about 9–10in in diameter at the hammer-end for a length of about 18in, after which it was reduced for the rest of the length of the shank to about 4–5in diameter. Up in the roof of the anchor-shop, the shank passed between a pair of grooved, belt-driven pulleys. These were spring-loaded so that they could grip the narrow shank of the beetle and lift it several feet up into the air (I have been told that in some cases the shank of the beetle actually passed out through the roof of the shop). A hammer-driver down below controlled the spring pressure by means of a rope, and as he pulled on the rope, the pressure of the two grooved rollers on the shaft was released and the heavy weight plunged down on to the part of the anchor where it was being welded, guided by a group of men using long iron hooks, which were similar to shepherds' crooks.

Bob Denholm remarked to me that some anchor smiths could be seen wearing hats, waistcoats and even overcoats while forging the anchors. He said that they were 'like the Arabs' in that they believed in the old saying that whatever keeps the cold out, keeps the heat out.

The anchor smiths carried out their work on a large round anvil, and close to one side of it was what was known as a 'tip hole'. This was normally covered over with iron plates, but when it became necessary to work on the side of the shank the anchor could be 'tipped over' and the arm dropped into the tip hole so that it was out of the way. At the same time as the arm was welded to the shank the square corner was filled with iron to form a strengthening radius. The last operation was the fitting of the shackle at the top of the shank on to which could be attached the cable-chain. The horseshoe-shaped shackle was usually placed over the end of the shank, and the whole lot lowered on to the hot pin (located on a flat anvil) that was to hold it in position, but allow movement of the shackle. Following the placing in position of a spacer ring over the hot pin, a team of men then descended on the projecting part of the pin and rained blows upon it from all points of the compass until it assumed a 'domed' shape and sealed the pin in position.

One-armed mooring anchors and some double-armed anchors also had a smaller shackle fitted at the opposite end to facilitate handling.

Developing Anchor Designs

There were several variations of the standard fixed-arm stock anchor, one being the Trotmans' anchor, which allowed the arms to pivot on a central pin in a slot at the bottom of the shank. Richard Perring, an Admiralty clerk at Plymouth Dockyard, suggested various improvements for anchors in his book published in 1819, one of which was that the arms of an anchor should be curved and not straight as they had been up to that time. However, examples of early Roman iron anchors have been discovered with curved arms and their design is very similar to anchors of the nineteenth century.

Very little information has been found on the methods used for bending or curving the arms on a stock or common anchor. Before the introduction of the steam hammer in the 1840s, it is possible that the bending was carried out using hand hammers and the beetle drop-hammer, with the added help of various blocks placed under one end to help with the bending. With the introduction of the steam hammer a certain amount of bend was put into the arm while it was being shaped under the hammer. The flukes were first fire-welded on to the arm, and then the arm was welded on to the shank. Bob Denholm told me that a 'screw-stretcher' was then used to pull the arm around to the desired radius. This was then checked by using a previously made template cut from thin sheet metal.

The 'screw-stretcher' was really a copy of the railway screw coupling; in fact on small jobs when the space was limited railway couplings were used. Bob Denholm mentioned, as an example, that during the bending of a batch of four 7in diameter shackles which had an inside diameter of 26in (destined for a steelworks), larger versions of the screw couplings were used. These sometimes had threads that were either square or pointed and could have a diameter of 2in. In the centre of the coupling was a block, which had a tommy-bar fitted through it, sometimes with knobs on the ends, for better handling. This block was fitted with two screwed rods, one with a left-hand thread and the other with a right-hand thread; the threaded rods passed through blocks that fitted in a shackle. As the centre block was rotated with the aid of the tommy-bar, the shackles closed in towards the centre. Attached to the shackles were lengths of chain, which were fitted to the ends of the object that was to be bent. This was a very powerful tool and, with the judicious help of heat and watering cans in appropriate places, the correct bend could be obtained.

In the eighteenth-century Royal Navy the rule of thumb in supplying anchors to ships was to allow 1cwt of anchors to each gun carried; this was

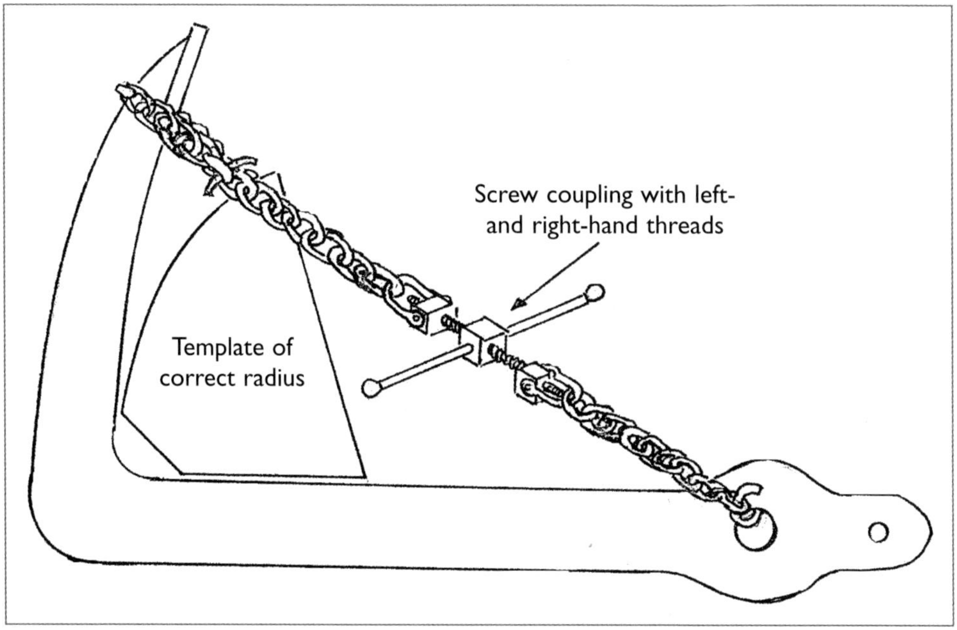

Pulling the arm of a single-arm anchor to its correct radius. *(Ron Moss)*

later changed to relate to the tonnage of the vessel. A merchant ship of 200 tons was typically equipped with anchors weighing 10cwt, and for every 100 tons' additional size 5cwt were added. This meant that a ship of 500 tons needed anchors weighing 25cwt. As ship displacements increased Lloyds Rules stated that this proportion did not apply, as a large ship did not need as great a proportion of weight of anchors as a smaller ship. Therefore we find that a vessel of 3,000 tons, which under the original calculation would need anchors weighing 150cwt, is tabled as only needing 128¼cwt.

The 'Modern' Stocked Anchor

By the nineteenth century the world's maritime nations had more or less standardised their anchors on the type with fixed forged iron arms and a wooden stock. An anchor of this type, preserved in its original condition, can be seen on HMS *Victory* in the Royal Navy's Portsmouth Dockyard.

By 1800 the Navy Board had received many complaints that anchors were breaking, quite often through the crown. Although it did not directly concern his department, Richard Perring took great interest and decided to investigate the problem. In January 1801 Perring put forward plans together with models for an anchor design that avoided welding the arms direct to the shank, but it was 1813 before the Admiralty was able to experiment with his design. One of the important things that Perring specified was the selection of properly refined iron in the form of flat-rolled bars. He also insisted on proper annealing to dark red after manufacture of the anchor and slow cooling. Although he was not a professional naval expert, but a book-keeper, he standardised the dimensions of anchors, in a range 1–95cwt, and he also specified suitable anchor equipment for sailing ships of 10–2,600 tons register.

Stockless Anchors

In about 1850, to allow anchors to be neatly stowed away, the stockless anchor was developed. Having no stock to get in the way the anchor could be drawn up tightly in the ship's hawse-hole. One consequence of this was to make the cathead (a marine crane) gradually obsolete, as stockless anchors gradually replaced most of the stocked anchors, though small stocked anchors are still manufactured today. The manufacture of the cathead was a complicated and specialist job and Walter Somers of Halesowen had the contract to make these for the Admiralty, and supplied them right up to 1898. Although steel was used by this time for the majority of jobs at the Walter Somers Haywood Forge, the Admiralty still specified wrought iron for the manufacture of catheads. The job of the cathead was to lift the anchor on to

The Queens

Most people are familiar with the story of the RMS *Titanic* because this brand new luxury liner sank with many of her passengers on her maiden voyage on a freezing cold night in April 1912. A growing number of interested people also know that much of the equipment for this vessel was manufactured in the Black Country which, for the 200-year period between 1770 and 1970, was one of the largest centres of engineering excellence in the country, an area that was described in many books as 'the workshop of the world'.

Not so much publicity is given to the fact that the area also supplied the fittings for many other famous Atlantic liners, which included the Cunard Queens. Many of the anchor chains and anchors for these great liners were forged in the Black Country and Noah Hingley of Netherton had the honour of supplying these for the *Titanic* but the anchoring equipment for the *Queen Mary* and *Queen Elizabeth* were supplied by another famous Black Country firm, Samuel Taylor of Brettell Lane, Brierley Hill. I was employed there as an electrical engineer at the time when the company also supplied the equipment for the royal yacht *Britannia*, working on the lifeboat davit recovery equipment. Part of the group included Welin Lambie

The anchor for the *Titanic* passing up Northfield Road, Netherton, on its way to Dudley LNWR station.

(known at that time as Welin McLaughlin Davits), which Samuel Taylor had taken over in 1931.

The 81,200-ton liner *Queen Mary* was supplied with Samuel Taylor's recently patented Tayco electrically welded high-tensile-steel anchor chain. It was 4⅛in diameter, and a length of 990ft of chain was supplied, each link measuring around 2ft long; three of Taylor's patented 'Dreadnought' anchors weighing 16 tons each completed the order.

An interesting story is related in the book *Atlantic Queens* (1989) by Clive Brooks regarding the naming of this great ship. Before the building of this ship Cunard had always given names to its ships ending in 'ia', as for example *Franconia*, *Saxonia*, *Caronia* and *Mauretania*, while its competitors, the White Star Line, gave its ships names ending in 'ic', as *Belgic*, *Britannic*, *Georgic* and *Titanic*.

The keel for an 80,000-ton liner was laid down in the John Brown shipyard at Clydebank in December 1930 and it appeared on the yard's books as 'Hull Number 534'. Then the interwar depression hit industry and the workers were sent home on 11 December 1931. The government of the day eventually decided that Number 534 should receive financial assistance from public funds to get the men back to work. Money to complete the ship was to be lent on favourable terms, but one of the conditions set was that Cunard merge with the White Star Line. At the end of March 1934 the men received notification to return to work.

Number 534 was completed and was ready to be launched on 30 September 1934. Meetings of representatives from the two companies must have ranged well into the night trying to come to an agreement as to what to name the ship; would it be a name ending in 'ic' or 'ia'? In the end it appears Cunard won because the name agreed upon was *Victoria*. The committee, however, did say that if it was decided to name the ship after a member of the royal family it would only be polite to ask permission from the present royal family. Lord Roydon, who was a personal friend of King George V, was detailed to ask royal permission and while out grouse shooting with the king he asked, 'Would His Majesty consent to the great liner being named after the most illustrious and remarkable woman who has ever been queen of England?' The king replied, 'That is the greatest compliment that has ever been made to me or my wife, I will ask her permission when I get home.' And so the great ship was named the *Queen Mary*. She left John Brown's shipyard on 3 March 1936.

Cunard's two Queens, the *Queen Mary* and the *Queen Elizabeth*, were famous throughout the world. They were great ambassadors for Britain. With their

This is the machine that was used to weld Tayco forged steel chain at the works of Samuel Taylor Brierley Hill. Shown on the machine is the 3in diameter chain that was supplied to the large luxury liners. A three-link piece of chain was taken from this length and tested at the Lloyds Proving House Netherton, on 4 November 1932. The test strain was increased until the chain broke at the remarkable load of 372.9 tons. It is interesting to compare it with the listed breaking strain for 3in wrought-iron cable-chain which is just over 204 tons. *(Thanks to Max Hill)*

decor, their tradition as luxury liners, their comfort and their efficiency, they were part of the greatest passenger fleet in the world, so it came as quite a shock to the world and especially to the hand-picked members of the crews when the chairman of Cunard White Star announced in November 1967 that both ships (along with three others, the *Caronia*, *Sylvania* and *Carinthia*) were going to be withdrawn from service and put up for sale. This was caused by the great reduction in the number of passengers using the ships and turning to aircraft for travelling, especially when crossing the Atlantic to and from the USA. The *Queen Elizabeth*, which had been modernised by the fitting of such things as air-conditioning and outdoor swimming pools in 1966, actually recorded increased passenger usage in 1968 after it had been announced that she was being withdrawn. One of the probable reasons was that people wanted a 'last fling', to sample luxury travel while it was still available.

The *Queen Mary* left Southampton for the last time on 31 October 1967 under the command of Captain Treasure Jones, having been bought by the city of Long Beach, California. During her long voyage the ship had to pass around Cape Horn, which gave the passengers a unique opportunity. Several London buses had been loaded aft of the main deck to be shipped to California so that future visitors to the ship could be transported from the centre of Long Beach to visit the ship. Passengers queued to take turns to board the buses so that they could tell their friends that they had travelled around Cape Horn on a London bus.

The *Queen Mary* arrived at the port of Long Beach, southern California, where she was to become a floating hotel and conference centre and form part of a collection of historic transport exhibits. Several years were spent preparing her for the millions of visitors who were to come aboard and marvel at the splendour of her decor. The remaining fuel was off-loaded, three of her four engines and three of her four propellers were removed and while in dry dock her underside was sand-blasted and painted. It was 1971 before the public were allowed to visit the ship. In all 8,000 tons of equipment was removed from her original 81,000 tons. This had to be compensated for, to enable the ship to settle down to her normal position in the water.

The newer and larger *Queen Elizabeth* did not fare so well. She left her home port of Southampton for the last time on 16 November 1968 and sailed for Florida, where she spent several months in Port Everglades. In 1970 in a bankruptcy sale she was purchased by a Chinese entrepreneur, C.Y. Yung, and she was sailed to Hong Kong where she was to be fitted out as a floating college and hotel to be known as the Seawise University. Unfortunately, with her refit well under way, she was engulfed by fire in Hong Kong harbour on 9 January 1972, a fire from which she never recovered.

Readers who want a really excellent account of the life of the Cunard Queens are recommended to consult the book *Atlantic Queens* by Clive Brooks, a must for any bookshelf.

the deck of the ship so that it could be secured, allowing the ship to put to sea.

The stockless anchor had pivoting arms and flukes attached to the shank, allowing it to dig into the sea bed. To help it in this task it also had a massive block of metal built into its design on the bottom of the arms, and this weight helped it to carry out its function of securing a ship on station.

Many designs of stockless anchor appeared, most of them made up of a set of parts. Many of these were made of cast steel, while others were forged from steel. The companies that made their stockless anchors by the forging method boasted in their publicity that the forged ones were superior to the cast ones because of the possibility of the presence of blow-holes in the castings, which tended to weaken them, whereas the hammering or forging of the metal tended to consolidate it.

Hall's patent stockless anchors, manufactured by such firms as Noah Hingley of Netherton, were fitted to some of the earlier large liners such as the *Titanic* while the later Queens were fitted with Samuel Taylor's Dreadnought anchors.

I owe thanks for much of the above information to Bob Denholm of Dudley Wood, Sydney Allen of Bromsgrove, John Dixon of Chester and Alan Hallman of Wordsley.

Hall's Patent Anchor

This anchor design was patented (No. 3461) by John Verity of Bromley, Leeds, and John Francis Hall of Norbury, Sheffield, in 1886, with two further patents taken out in 1888 and 1889. The clever idea of this patent was that the head swivelled through a limited angle on a trunnion passing through the shank. The original function of the stock was to turn the anchor so that a fluke entered the ground, but in this design the swivelling head carried out this task, helped by tripping pieces on the crosshead. The great advantage was that the absence of the stock allowed the anchor to be drawn right up into the hawse-pipe on the ship.

Before the introduction of the stockless anchor, coming to anchor was a long, laborious process. Normally stocked anchors were stowed and lashed on the forecastle or on the side of the ship and had to be moved into position when preparing to anchor. With the stockless anchor, the windlass gear was released, usually by knocking the locking peg out, and the anchor simply dropped by gravity.

Hall's anchor achieved almost instant success and was quickly taken up by shipping companies. The Admiralty quickly submitted it to a number of trials and it was soon adopted by the Royal Navy.

The 16-ton bow anchor for the *Titanic* standing in the yard of Lloyds of Netherton ready to move to Dudley station. Attached to the wagon are the eight Hingley horses selected for the job.

Several large firms in the Black Country had the capacity to manufacture these new stockless anchors. Very quickly on the scene was the world famous Netherton firm of Noah Hingley & Sons. They signed an agreement with Hall & Verity in July 1891 to manufacture Hall's Patent Anchor. Hingleys supplied many ships with these anchors, two of the most notable being the White Star liners *Olympic* and *Titanic.*

The large bow anchor of the *Titanic,* weighing around 16 tons, was secured not with the usual cable-chain but with a large wire hawser of 9½in circumference. This was supplied by Bullivant & Co. of London. The two side bower anchors, of 7½ tons each, were secured and worked with cable-chains, 330 fathoms long of 3¼in diameter, weighing in all 96 tons. Around ten fires at the Noah Hingley works in Netherton manufactured this anchor chain.

Whenever I see the often reproduced photograph of the large *Titanic* bow anchor being transported from the Lloyds' Proof House at Netherton up Cradley Road towards the town of Netherton hauled by twenty large horses,

I recall the story told to me by several Hingley's men about that day. Apparently the large wagon arrived at Lloyds hauled by twelve horses. The Hingley family were specially fond of their horses and used them for hauling loads both inside and outside the works long after most other firms had replaced them with steam traction engines. Most of the horses were fine specimens and weighed at least a ton each. One of the Hingley family, who was present in the yard when the wagon and horses arrived, is reported to have said, 'You can take those poor specimens off the wagon and put eight of our horses in their place. They will handle it easily.' The man in charge of the wagon pleaded for his horses to be harnessed on to the front of the Hingley horses because he had to get them back to their LNWR stables in Great Bridge that day.

And so the photograph shows twenty horses hauling the load up Cradley Road, and of course every writer using that photograph since has thought how thrilling that twenty horses were required to haul the *Titanic* anchor to

Two large Dreadnought anchors that were manufactured for the Cunard *Queen Mary* by Samuel Taylor Brierley Hill.

Dudley LNWR railway goods station for onward despatch to Fleetwood, and thence by ship to Northern Ireland.

The 'anchor attachments' for these liners, and many other ships, were for many years made by a gang of highly skilled smiths, many of the members of this crew emanating from the Denholm family. The attachments usually consisted of three large links made from iron that was larger than the cable-chain-links and joined the anchor to the cable-chain by means of shackles. In the case of the two White Star liners mentioned, these links were made out of 5½in and 6in diameter iron; the outside length of the links varied between 33in and 36in long.

Another Black Country firm, Samuel Taylor & Sons of Brierley Hill, was responsible for supplying the chains and anchors for the Cunard White Star luxury liners *Queen Mary* and *Queen Elizabeth* and, a little later, the royal yacht *Britannia*, among other ships.

The very popular anchor that Samuel Taylor supplied to many customers was known as the Dreadnought anchor. This was the anchor, together with patent Tayco chain, that was supplied to these famous liners. The anchors were forged, using large steam hammers, on Taylor's premises a mile outside Brierley Hill on the road towards Stourbridge, which were nicely situated for transport facilities between the Great Western Railway line at Brettell Lane and the Stourbridge Canal that ran right next to the works.

Another local firm, H.P. Parkes of Tipton, in 1867, supplied a new anchor, weighing 8 tons, and having a length of 20ft for use on Brunel's *Great Eastern*. At that time it was the largest anchor in the world.

In 1905 Lloyds published a list of 47 British firms that made approved patent anchors; 14 of these were located in the Black Country. By 1924 the same region was left with only 5 anchor-smith firms. Steel rapidly replaced wrought iron in anchor manufacture but it was 1979 before the last wrought-iron anchor-makers, Isaiah Preston of Cradley Heath, finally closed.

Many firms produced the standard traditional stocked anchor listed in catalogues as 'Admiralty', 'Kedge' or 'Common' anchor. Many firms also produced their own version of the 'stockless' anchor, usually having a heavy forged head. Another anchor, known from its shape as the 'mushroom anchor', was produced by most firms from around 1870. This was used mainly for anchoring on a permanent basis in soft and muddy conditions, and was especially popular for lightships and similar vessels.

A large stockless anchor is set up on a concrete plinth by the side of the canal near Owen Street bridge in Tipton as a reminder of the works of Joseph Wright & Co. Wright's Neptune Forge manufactured chain and anchors for many years and was located nearby.

Index

Allen, Sydney 15, 29, 31
Anchors:
  Common 121, 137
  Dreadnought 124, 134, 137
  Hall's Patent 134
  Kedge 123, 137
  Mushroom 137
  Noah Hingley 65
  Samuel Taylor 131, 133, 134
  Single arm 126
Apprenticeships 40, 42, 44, 47
Asea-Svets Co. 117

Babies 48, 49, 50, 51
Barnsley, John 101
Beetle drop-hammer 126, 127
Bellows 55, 67
'Benny Fiddler' 30
Black Country 12, 15, 16, 17, 19, 25, 28, 69, 91
Black Country Museum 12
Black Country Society 105
Bloomer, Noah 23, 24
Board of Trade 17, 59, 92
Boulton & Watt 21
Breeze 69
Brewhouse chain-shops 34, 40, 51, 55, 56, 63, 70, 103
Brierley Hill 64, 137
British Standards 86, 87
British Machine Made Chain Co. 112
Bronze chain 112
Brooks, Clive 131, 133
Brown-Lenox, Pontypridd 64, 70, 85, 102, 115
Brown, Samuel 14, 81, 85, 99
Brunton, Thomas 26, 99

Carousel method 111, 116
Cathead 129
Chain:
  Cable 11, 14, 26, 27, 28, 81, 86, 105, 112
  Dollied (end-welded) 82, 83, 84
  Electro-welded 17, 18, 40, 60, 98
  Machine-made 40, 107, 108, 109, 110
  Mooring 34
  Side-welded 18, 34, 68, 69, 79, 80, 81, 97, 102, 103, 104
  Small, hammered 32, 34, 40, 42, 105
  Square 6, 22, 25, 26
  Tommied (end-welded) 24, 79, 81, 109, 110, 111
  Twisted 27, 50
Chained libraries 4, 5
Chain-shops 15, 16, 17, 34, 61, 62, 63, 66, 67, 71
Chain test 34, 61, 88
Children in chain-shops 34, 35, 47, 51, 52, 53, 54, 85
Churchill, Winston 36
Cradley Heath 15, 16, 17, 29, 30, 31, 34, 37, 39, 55
Crowley, Ambrose 9, 48, 49
Cunard Line 116, 122, 130–3, 137

Defence chains 8, 9, 10, 11
Denholm family 64, 65, 66, 90, 91, 121, 127, 137
Dobbin 56
Dolly tools 54, 81, 82, 83, 84
Domestic chain-shops 35
Dreadnought anchor 124, 136
Dudley 30, 63, 105

Early anchors 4, 5, 6, 8
Early chains 6, 7, 8
Electrically welded chain 40
Eliza Tinsley & Co. 59, 78
End links 96

Fuel used 69

Galsworthy, John 39
Germany 90, 91
Griff-Chains 68, 110
Griffin, William & Sons 105
Griffin Woodhouse Ltd 105, 106, 107
Guest, Walter 106

Hancock's chain 20, 21
Harland & Wolff, Belfast 112
Health & Safety at Work 47
Hearths 75, 76
Hemp cable 11, 12, 13, 26, 86, 87, 88
Henry Wood & Co. 18, 54, 55, 81, 95, 102, 121, 124, 125
Holden & Hunt, Old Hill 110
Hours worked 40

Indentures 44, 45
Industrial Archaeology Group, B.C.S. 105
Inspectors 51, 80
Integral-stud chain 105, 106, 107
Iron 13, 14

John Brown, Clydebank 131
Johnny hammer 103, 122
Joining the link 78
Jones & Lloyd 45, 55

Kenter shackle 118

Lists, price of chain 46
Lloyds, Brierley Hill 116, 118
Lloyds Register 85, 86, 90, 91, 94, 129, 135, 137
Lock-out of 1910 36, 39, 40

Macarthur, Mary 32, 36, 37, 38, 39
Metal used 14, 6, 88
Middlemen 35
Mine-anchoring chain 82
Minesweeper chain 112
Minimum wage 32, 35
Monday hammer 3
Mushroom Green 56, 58, 66, 68, 75, 80, 104, 110

Nailing 22, 52, 74
National Federation of Women Workers 36
Noah Bloomer 62, 68, 83
Noah Hingley, Netherton 28, 47, 70, 80, 82, 88, 100, 101, 102, 104, 105, 112, 113, 117, 120

Old Hill 43, 50, 51, 57, 62, 70, 78
Oliver 72, 73, 77
Outworkers 55, 56, 59, 60

Parkes, H.P., Tipton 81, 137
Pardoe, Mrs 105
Patrimony 47
Piecework 43
Plot, Robert 48, 77

Position of join or weld 78, 79, 81
Preston, Isaiah, Cradley Heath 137
Price lists 33, 46
Proving Establishments 14, 85, 88, 92

Quakers 48
Queen liners 116, 118, 122, 130–3, 134, 136

Rattle chain 19, 22, 25, 44
Rods 56
Rolled bar 25
'Roland for an Oliver' 74
Roman anchors 4, 7
Ropes 2, 3, 8, 11, 12, 13
Royal Navy 14, 34, 84, 85, 88, 93, 105, 128
Rylett, Harold 45, 51

Samuel Taylor & Co. 87, 111, 113, 118, 124, 130, 136
Shackles 64, 66, 88, 118
Sitch, Tom 38
Slave chains 12, 13
Standard chain sizes 86, 95, 96
Stevens, Harry 43
Stockless anchor 129, 134
Strathern, A.G., Gartsherrie 109
Spinners End 31
Spring pole 73, 79
Stourbridge 48
Strikes 31
Stone anchors 6, 119
Studs 26, 81, 83, 99, 100, 101, 102, 105
Sykes, Sir Richard 88

Tawney, R.H. 16, 17
Tayco chain 113, 114, 115, 116, 117, 118, 132
Test certificates 34, 61, 89, 91, 93
Testing 14, 85, 87, 88, 89, 92, 94, 96, 97, 98
Titanic anchor and chains 6, 66, 101, 112, 113, 130, 135
Tommy hammer 23, 35, 62, 63, 74, 75, 76, 78, 79
Tommy shops 78
Trade Boards 71
Trade Board Acts 35
Traill, Thomas 13, 17, 79, 89
Tools, anchor 44, 72
Trotman's anchor 123, 127

Unions 15, 25, 28, 30, 31, 33, 35, 38, 46, 90

Wages in chain trade 32, 34, 38, 39, 40
Walter Somers Haywood Forge 129
Weldless steel chain 109
Welin davits 131
White Star Line 101, 102, 137
Wilkinson, John 19, 20
Wire rope 25
Woodhall, Lucy 40, 41, 109
Women chain-makers 34, 35, 40, 43, 50
Women's Trade Union League 36, 38
Woodhouse, Joseph 110, 112
Woodhouse, Henry 102, 104
Woodhouse, Samuel 40, 41, 60, 106
Woodhouse, Wilson 110
Woodhouse Bros 105
Wright, Joseph 137
Wrought iron 13, 14, 19, 22

Young children 35